D1170807

How to Make Your Own Greeting Cards

JOHN CARLIS

How to Make Your Own Greeting Cards

Watson-Guptill Publications
New York

Published 1968 in New York by Watson-Guptilll Publications,
a division of Billboard Publications, Inc.,
165 West 46 Street, New York, N.Y.

Manufactured in the U.S.A.
ISBN 0-8230-2425-3
Library of Congress Catalog Card Number: 68-27549
First Printing, 1968
Second Printing, 1970
Third Printing, 1972

for Mabel Williams Garrison

Acknowledgments

I would like to thank the many friends who sent examples of greetings they had designed and produced, and to especially thank Susan Meyer and James Craig of Watson-Guptill — Miss Meyer for her generous and enormous assistance in simplifying and classifying a mass of material; Mr. Craig for a distinguished format for the text and sketches.

Contents

Introduction

If you have the urge to make your own greeting cards, you may be thinking, "But I don't even know how to *draw*." You don't have to. Or you might say, "Actually, I'm a rather good draftsman, but I'd like to do something a little more interesting than just hand the printer a sketch to print."

Whether you're merely a doodler, a Sunday painter, or a real pro, this book shows you how to design and *graphically reproduce* an original idea of your own, in quantities from a couple of dozen to several hundred. "They smiled when I sat down to my work table, but when they received my Christmas card, they really stood up and cheered!" And why shouldn't they? Each card will be an *original, signed work of art*. Whether it's a small monotype, radiant with gem-like color, a smart box fold decoupage, a subtle tempera batik, or even a wild broadside that unfolds to 24″, you can bet your boots there won't be another one like it on any of your friends' mantles or library tables!

We send greeting cards mainly because, in this jet age, *letter writing* is a lost art. Years ago, current events elicited the leisurely comments of our parents and grandparents in long letters that needed days or weeks for delivery; now these events are seen by all the world hourly on television. If cousin Ethel has had an appendectomy, we no longer spend an afternoon composing a letter filled with local news and several new jokes calculated to cheer her up. Two thousand miles may separate us, but we'll *both* turn to the world news on tv, and then perhaps to the same comedy team, immediately after dinner.

So we *telephone* cousin Ethel, long distance, with an eye on our watch for the three-minute time limit. Or we spend three minutes of our very precious lunch hour choosing a card in a card shop. Or (and that's why you have this book in hand), we simply sign something we've made ourselves and quickly slip it into an envelope with an air mail stamp, confident that she'll be opening the envelope in a very short while.

Invitations, cards for convalescents, birthday and anniversary cards, *bon voyage* cards, sympathy cards, Valentine cards, and birth announcements can be every bit as much fun to make as Christmas or Easter cards — and are even more of a surprise. Once you've settled on the idea and reproduced it a couple of dozen times, you have a unique group of thoughtful remembrances all ready to send. And a card you've designed and made yourself will be every bit as personal as a letter *ever* could have been.

Some cards attractively mounted — as simple as dried leaves or flowers or photograms — can serve a wide variety of occasions. And a quantity of cards like these can be made, almost without effort, while you're enjoying radio or television. On the other hand, a monotype, an etching, a set of carefully hand colored Xerox prints, will all need your full attention. No matter how simple or elaborate your card, I'll wager you're going to have a great deal of enjoyment cutting, pasting, stamping, tracing, batiking, blotting.

When you have something to show (on a card, naturally), will you drop me a line, c/o my publisher? I'd be delighted to hear from you at Watson-Guptill Publications, 165 West 46 Street, New York, New York 10036.

All right, let's roll up our sleeves and get to work!

1

Ideas, and Where to Find Them

The cards you probably want to make will run the gamut from religious holidays to all sorts of everyday needs. Popular symbols and motifs for Christmas, Easter, Rosh Hoshanah, and Hannukah can easily be found in newspaper advertising or magazine illustrations. Art books — especially museum publications — offer a wealth of inspiration. And what about your own sketchbook? You may have sketched or photographed a particular spire, dome, stained glass window, or candlestick which could be a starting point for your design.

Using Quotations

Quotations, with the lettering forming some imaginative pattern, can be used for Christmas or birthday greetings; for *bon voyage* or get well cards; for any occasion at all, providing the quotation is to the point. A look into Bartlett's *Familiar Quotations* might give you just the line you're looking for. Here's a list of books you might check at your local library:

Businessmen's Book of Quotations by R. L. Woods, 1951, McGraw-Hill.
Familiar Quotations by John Bartlett, 1955, Little, Brown.
5,000 Quotations for All Occasions by Lewis C. Henry, 1956, Doubleday.
Home Book of Bible Quotations by Burton Stevenson, 1956, Dodd, Mead.
Home Book of Catholic Quotations by John Chapin, 1956, Farrar, Straus.
Home Book of Shakespeare Quotations by Burton Stevenson, Scribner.
Oxford Dictionary of Quotations, 1955, Oxford University Press.
Pocket Book of Quotations by Henry Davidoff, 1952, Pocket Books.
Treasury of Jewish Quotations by J. L. Baron, 1956, Crown.

Perhaps an advertising slogan would do the trick neatly; you might simply cut it out of the newspaper and create a "setting" of colored papers for it!

For a Valentine, you might choose a favorite line of poetry or even an entire sonnet, illustrating it with a drawing or decoration of your own, or perhaps with a print. A lyric from a popular musical might work well for congratulations; I'm sure we've all seen the commercial card that reads, "I could have danced all night!"

Let Your Imagination Run Wild

Let's go back to Christmas. Take snow. Think of *all* the things you can do with this one idea! Snowmen, snowballs, snowflakes, snowdrifts, *snowstorms*. There you are: Whittier's poem, "Snowbound." Perhaps you can reprint it inside a fold of midnight blue suede paper; lay a 3" or 4" plastic snowflake on the cover as a stencil (see the shopping guide at the back of the book for suede paper and plastic snowflakes); and give it a quick diagonal spray with canned "snow" (your supermarket will have this). Lift the plastic snowflake off, and do the next one.

You can think of lots of things relating to Christmas. Take some typical symbols: Candle, or Front Door with Wreath, or Lighted Tree. Make a drawing of each of these *three times*. Make your first drawing with a laundry marker; follow this up with Junior's crayons; then try drawing with brush and ink on whatever colored paper you can find around the house.

You'll now have nine sketches of Candle, nine sketches of Front Door with Wreath, nine sketches of Lighted Tree. You're bound to see something you want to use in *one* of those twenty-seven sketches; if you don't, your wife (or husband or sister) surely will. They'll say, "Dear, why don't you put one of the silver sequins *there*, or a line *here*, or a touch of color *there*." And you'll be on your way!

Hobbies

A friend of mine draws birds, and puts birds on his cards. Always birds. Well, he's a good bird drawer, but he wasn't *always* a good bird drawer. He started out drawing what he *claimed* was a "robin flying South" for some friends going to Florida one winter. His friend's wife took the card out of the envelope and said it was the wildest robin she'd ever seen; she laughed so hard we had a rough time getting her on the plane. Later she enlarged the design, and made a hooked rug out of it; a reminder of annual trips, the crudely lettered legend, "Gonna spread my wings and fly away," is faithfully copied in black yarn. The whole idea went over so well that the so-called "robin" is my friend's trademark on all his cards.

Museums and Libraries

Try to collect assortments of postcards from museum bookshops. Filed in a small drawer, they offer quick reference and are not only easier to use than a book page (for tracing etc.), but can also be mounted on a fold of colored or decorative paper. Masterpieces of painting and sculpture offer inspiration for you, but don't neglect the decorative arts collections — the necklaces, tiles, silver, furniture. You might find an Irish crosier or staff you'd sketch for St. Patrick's day or a photo enlargement of a Roman cameo — with a design of a lion — to make a birthday card for a friend born under the sign of Leo. For friends who are interested in astrology, make short condensations of the chief characteristics of all twelve signs of the zodiac. Newspapers and magazines print these frequently. (For example, see *McCall's*, June, 1967.) Carbon or Hectograph copies of your condensation inside a folder with *your own* design of a ram, a bull, a lion, or a fish on the cover will make a very personal greeting.

During the years I designed and produced greeting cards for a number of stores, I took from my postcard files, one morning, a fantasy eighteenth century Florentine cabinet and wall sconce, and added a sleeping cat on a chair. Having designed it as a Valentine, I then wrote the following rhyme:

By candlelight, a sleeping cat
Is unaware of my affection
As you are of my fondest wish
To add my heart to your collection!

The cabinet carried Valentines on the shelves and there were hearts for drawer pulls; it sold very well, as I recall. Printed by commercial offset in gray, cerise, and blue, the little cabinet and sleeping cat unit — with its appropiate border — was cut out of the sheet and "tipped" or pasted at the top to a piece of silver foil. These pieces of foil were then "tipped" again onto a rougher textured fold of pink paper, with the greeting added inside, in terracotta ink. The jug, the rug, the doorway, or the Staffordshire figurine *you* find might be handled similarly, with your sketch reproduced on your office Xerox machine and color added by hand. Or perhaps a drypoint (see page 85) cut into plastic would be more suitable for your subject matter.

Museums also offer splendid displays, which you can sketch or even photograph: magnificent arrangements of greenery, with a work of art at a focal point; sweeps of staircases; patios, courtyards, and fountains, all with architectural stonework which can be useful to you. The toys from all over the world sold at museum shops are fun to collect, as are the inexpensive reproductions of jewelry and small sculptures; all these can be starting points for your cards.

And you don't have to live in a big city to enjoy museum *membership*. Even if you live in a mountain village (as I once did in California), the postman can bring you beautiful books and exciting pieces of printed matter from any museum you choose, throughout the year, for about what you'd pay for a pair of slacks.

Libraries are a rich source of ideas: they have all the art books you need; they probably have a twenty-five cent photostat copying machine nearby; they also have an endless amount of literary quotations. Magazine articles can be tracked down through the library's *Readers' Guide to Periodical Literature*. If your local library doesn't have the particular issue you need of *Holiday*, *House & Garden*, or *Field & Stream*, you can write directly to a backdate magazine service.

I find the microfilm files of newspapers, now in all libraries across the country, enormously stimulating. A turn of the little wheel gives you the news of former days, and shows all the advertising on the day you were born, carries the excitement of the laying of the first transatlantic cable, of Peary at the North Pole, or of Lindbergh's flight to Paris. Like the museums, many libraries now have shops where postcard reproductions and books are sold, and recurrent exhibitions of book treasures and works of art can offer you inspiration. The constantly expanding shelves of books for children offer both amusing quotations and bright, new color suggestions, as well as new ideas for painting, drawing, and printing techniques.

Television

The magic box that lights up is loaded with ideas you can photograph directly and adapt as you choose. When the commercials bore you, you can sit there and think, "But what can I find here that's a good idea for a card?" If the *program* bores you, naturally you can think the same thing. Let's say that a pair of well known comedians are shown in a studio orange grove, standing on ladders, picking oranges. Suddenly, they start *throwing* the oranges at one another. It happens not to strike you as particularly funny, but you think, "Oranges, apples, orange juice, *orange juice!*" So you think of the old pun: "Orange juice ever going to write me?" Then you either sketch a glass of orange juice or cut one out of a magazine. You letter the words "orange juice" above the glass and then add, inside the fold, "ever going to write to me?" All right, maybe it's corny, so try a pun of your own.

One evening, not long ago, I watched night falling over the city. As all the signs began blinking on the tops of various buildings, I wrote these lines for a birthday card, using a city skyline at dusk for the illustrations:

I would this birthday wish were set
A circuit of bright waves of light
High on some city parapet
To flash "Good Morning!" and "Good Night!"
Then all the town would join in cheers
And loudly call your happy name
Good Fortune for the future years
Admission to the Hall of Fame!

Let me be the first to admit it isn't great poetry, but I'll use it for a birthday card anyway, and if you think you'd like to use it, too, go ahead!

A design for an anniversary greeting might be inspired by something as mundane as a television news report showing an excavation for a new building. In your sketch or print, you might show a close-up of part of the excavating, with the line inside reading: "We dig you two the most!"

Suppose your television screen shows a cartoon of a rocket, and you need a Valentine idea. There it *is*, right in front of you: "You send me into outer space, Baby!" If you can't draw a rocket, get your nephew to do it for you. Or practice; learn to draw *your own* kind of rocket.

Motion Picture Ideas

Just as electronics has made it possible for us today to sit in a chair and *hear* any sound or any music ever made on earth, we can also — through the means of the motion picture — *see* just about anything ever created on this planet by nature or by man — or indeed, in the heavens. Take the movie credits, for example. An unprecedented store of visual material is constantly being used by the designers of the credits, or titles, of motion pictures. So the cloud patterns or cave paintings, the ancient scrolls, or modern typewriter keys that will help create the screen credits you are watching might be the "kick off" for the greeting card idea you need. It's as simple as that.

A number of recent motion picture titles, notably those for the James Bond films, have been outstanding for their use of intense and fluid semi-abstract washes of color moving into new and startling shapes. These abstractions are usually drawn from original photographic shots of figures.

If you mix some bright oil colors with enough turpentine to allow you to pour the colors separately and float them on the surface of a basin of water, you can have some fun. You can create a fluid pattern of your own for marbleized card paper by drawing a comb or a jagged edge of cardboard over the surface of the floating thinned paint, making a decorative pattern. Drop a sheet of white or colored paper over the paint and lift up quickly. A design any professional would envy will be the result!

Similarly, the audacious use of typography in motion picture titles — one or two words filling the entire screen, or reduced to a mere nothing in one corner — might suggest ways of using certain *words* as *pictorial matter* in a greeting. Study the use of stripes and bands which are charged with color, and consider the logic of the strategically placed spot or symbol. Photograms — discussed in Chapter 12 — are frequently used in titles. Watch for the use of such textures as lace or velvet; the surfaces of brick, stone, or wooden walls, as well as wrought iron grill work and clipped hedges. All these devices, used in motion picture titles, can provide you with ideas.

So, if duty insists you go along to a movie on an evening when you'd rather stay home, cheer up! Perhaps the titles will offer you more food for thought than the film itself!

Printed Advertising

Lots of automobile ads, with their printed slogans, can make real zingy one-of-a-kind greetings very suitable for a wide variety of needs. For example: On the outside of the card you can paste "Pontiacs come with Trophy V-8 power (the kind that answers when you call)." On the inside you can letter, "So be my Pontiac!"

Cut out a telephone from one ad, a car from another. Arrange these as a montage, perhaps using another picture you've found, and paste them down on a fold of colored paper. Sign, address, and mail the card. Again, "Kellogg's Corn Flakes are Dandy," and inside: "But we're going to have *Steaks* at our Cook Out Saturday, the 20th. Please let us know if you can join us." For the same barbecue party, you might send other friends a card illustrated by pictures of parachutists, and the slogan, "Where the Action Is," writing inside: "At our Saturday Night Barbecue—that's where. Can you come?"

If you run across a picture in your morning paper that you'd like to cut in linoleum, try this system. Lay the cut-out picture face down on the block, and wet the back of the paper with lighter fluid, a solution that will transfer the printer's ink to your linoleum if you briskly rub down the wet newsprint with the bowl of a spoon. Be sure that the picture you select has a distinct line you can follow with your linocutting tool.

Be a Pop artist; carefully cut a picture of a can of soup, and paste it within a quickly sketched watercolor frame. Write on the card, "Whoops! I'm in the Soup! I forgot your Birthday!" Be daring. For "The Skin You Love to Touch," add; "Would that I *could!*" Be sentimental; cut out "Say it with Flowers," using the printed flowers in the ad as well as the slogan, or create a bouquet of your own, adding "Happy Anniversary." I think you get the idea.

Decorating Ideas

In the following chapters, I'm going to describe lots of methods of reproducing greeting cards. You can combine these methods or use them individually, as you please. The variations are endless. Regardless of the technique you use, you might find some of the following suggestions for decorating your cards helpful in adding a certain spark to the design.

Flocking

Flocking can produce the effects of velvet, fur, or suede—a tactile quality which adds a pleasing dimension. Flock is cotton or wool waste which has been pulverized and dyed. You can apply it to your Easter bunny to produce a nice, furry coat; or you can get a look of real mohair on the easy chair in which you've sketched Father for a Father's Day card. Flock is available in packages at art materials stores. To apply the flock, follow these directions studying Figures 1-3.

In a saucer, mix one part Elmer's Glue-All to one part water. Next, dip a dabber (a rag tied in a knot) into the saucer of adhesive, and dab your printing block with diluted white glue or—if you're not printing from a block—paint the design with the glue solution. Print the block onto the paper, using a minimum of pressure. Then put one or two tablespoons of the flock into a tea strainer, and sift this over the printed adhesive. When the glue is dry, shake off any surplus flock.

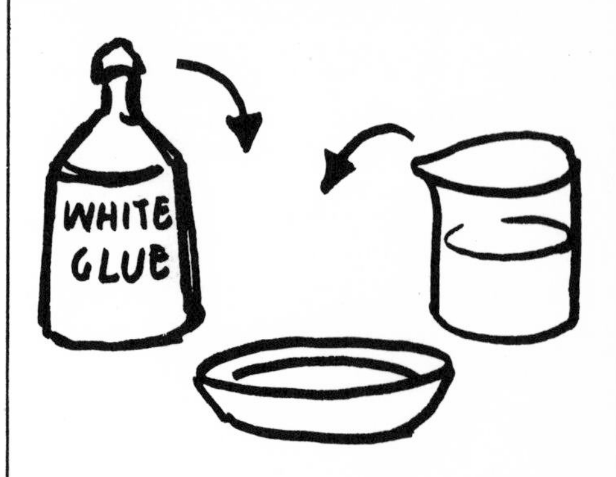

1. *Mix one part Elmer's Glue-All to one part water.*

2. *Dip a dabber into the saucer of adhesive and dab the printing surface with the diluted white glue.*

3. *Put one or two tablespoons of flock into a tea strainer and sift it over the printed adhesive.*

Flitter

Flitter — minute flakes of plastic — gives your cards the effect of diamond or gold dust; it comes in silver and a wide range of colors, including chartreuse, crimson, light turquoise, and midnight blue which you might want to use for glamor on some of your cards. For glittering candelabra, a lush theatrical curtain, or a Mardi Gras costume that you want to really shine, flitter will fill the bill. You'll find flitter at art materials stores, stocked with supplies for sign writers.

To apply flitter, first prepare a saucer of adhesive as you would for flock (one part Elmer's Glue-All to one part water). Dab the adhesive on the stamping block and print the adhesive, or paint the glue solution directly onto the design. Then allow the adhesive to set for a moment until it gets tacky, but not dry. Place the print inside the lid of a cardboard box (see Figure 4) so that you can retain excess flitter. Pour the flitter directly from a jar or paper cup over the tacky glue. When the glue is completely dry, your cards will sparkle. Pour the surplus flitter out of the box lid back into the storage jar (Figure 5).

4. *Place the print inside the lid of a cardboard box and pour the flitter directly from a jar or paper cup over the tacky glue.*

5. *Pour the surplus flitter out of the box lid back into the storage jar.*

Ornamented Tips

A *tip* is anything pasted onto your original greeting card which acts as an accent. The Dennison shops (see shopping guide) sell little boxes of the gold and silver stars used by music teachers, red or silver signal dots, notarial seals, and red bordered labels used by offices. Ten cent stores sell packets of silver, gold, and colored sequins, as well as glass tubes of imitation diamonds, rubies, and pearls. Be sure to get the kind of rhinestones that are flat on the back so you can paste them down. Bits of ribbon, ready-made bows, and tiny sprigs of flowers sold by millinery suppliers are excellent tips. Artificial shamrocks, holly, and mistletoe can also be found at millinery suppliers, as well as such diverse plastic miniatures as frolicking lambs and old-fashioned telephones. Items like these are advertised in the classified directories of the larger cities.

You can buy elaborately embossed and die-cut Viennese gold paper borders and ornaments from Brandon Memorabilia (see shopping guide) or from Harrower House of Découpage (see shopping guide). Most of these gold paper ornaments come with a good many units together on a 5" x 6" page, so one or two sheets should be all you need.

Additional Hints

Relax, be cool; the big thing to remember in the Idea Department is to be loose, to be free, to be alert, *and to have fun.* Having fun can be just putting together some colors you like and adding a single word, again cut from an ad. Don't they say that brevity is the soul of wit? And *ads* are where all the pretty typefaces are.

Don't worry about academic notions concerning color schemes, but *do* try to have a Light, a Dark, and a Bright Color. For texture, try to have a Rough, a Smooth, and a Slick. Just as a good chef subconsciously thinks hot, cold, sweet, sour, bland, and sharp as he plans a menu, you'll want your design to have varied weight and punch in its color and texture. So you'll paste a shiny and slick, brightly colored photograph on a rectangle of *dull* gold, mounting these in turn on a rougher surfaced, very dark green, dark blue, or maroon background. Perhaps a simpler illustration would be a vigorous linoleum cut printed in sharp black on crisp white paper, with a touch of scarlet added.

The view from your window can provide ideas for your cards. A poem was written inside to suit the occasion. By John Carlis.

Printed advertising, used cleverly, can make real one-of-a-kind greetings. This ad came from a magazine, ideal for an invitation to a barbeque. By John Carlis.

The idea for this card came from a postcard of an eighteenth century Florentine cabinet and wall sconce. The cat was added and an appropriate poem written. By John Carlis.

Here is a clever idea: combining the music for a Christmas carol with the American flag. Derek Norman and Family. Collection, Dione Guffey.

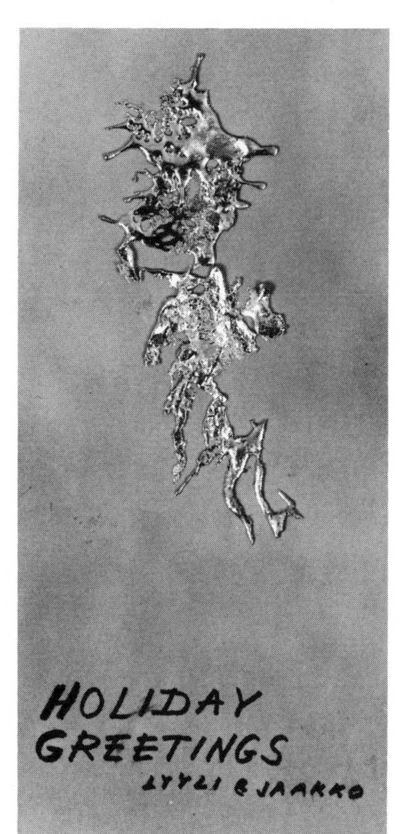

To produce a lively, accidental three dimensional effect, you can dribble melted lead—or even a thick glue like sobo—on your card. By Jaakko Hurme.

A silk-screened stocking provides an unusual Christmas greeting. By Kramer, Miller, Lomden, Glassman.

"Make your own Santa!" You can create something like this assembly kit and Xerox copies for all your friends. By Landis.

The artist pasted four pictures of himself into this 19th century engraving. With a little color in the costumes, he added interest to the card. By Frank Skorski.

2

Paper, Folds, and Envelopes

Paper is part of the picture. This is a slogan of one of the paper manufacturers, and it's certainly true: paper is a *very big* part of the picture. So plan on dressing up your greeting card idea as carefully as you would dress yourself for a special occasion. Maybe this chapter may give you some ideas for your greeting cards.

Selecting Papers

In paper, the wide range of colors alone can inspire you. For example, in the ten cent stores, there are inexpensive packs of colored construction paper which contain pinks, mauves, grays, and tans found nowhere else. And since the weight of these sheets is good both for printing *and* folding most cards, you might want to have one or two packages of this inexpensive paper on hand to use for your first printing experiments. (Most construction papers have a tendency to fade after a time, but this feature is hardly a drawback for a greeting card.)

After you've experimented in construction paper, you can ask your art supplier to show you other papers: soft Japanese rice papers; various watercolor sheets; the somewhat harder charcoal papers in their delicate tints; Color Aid sheets, with their amazing range of numbered colors. There are papers with oatmealy textures that come in white, ivory, tan, pink, pale green, lilac, and pale blue. Watch for special sales in the stationery section of department stores; sometimes you can find boxes of writing paper with matching envelopes attractively lined.

Strathmore Beau Brilliant—a sheet as elegant as its name—comes in beautiful deep, rich colors. Strathmore Double Deckle carries a color on one side of a 25″ x 35″ sheet with the same color in a lighter tint on the reverse side. A ⅜″ band of the darker tone ornaments the "deckle" (the torn, feathery, long edges) on the tint side of this sheet. Be sure to buy samples of Strathmore Silverflake and Goldflake as well as one or two sheets of the vellums and parchments. (Ask for a heavy parchment called "Elephant Hide.")

Metallic papers—in shiny or dull silver or gold, or in colors—and aristocratic suede papers can make splendid mountings for your prints. But also experiment with tinted mimeograph paper, cheap sulphite butcher, and brown and gray kraft papers, and with the many colors of flint glazed box-covering papers. Get a sample of Pellon, the paper stiffening material sold at dressmakers' supply counters in department stores.

I've printed cards on gift wrapping paper, on wallpaper, and even on fine sandpaper! Perhaps your design will work best as a blueprint or a brownprint bought from a commercial blueprinter who will work from your original sketch on tracing paper (see Chapter 12). For a *bon voyage* card you might want to use part of a page of a foreign language newspaper, either as printing paper or a folder. In fact, there are designers who avoid paper *altogether,* and send out ultra modern cards printed on sheets of clear or colored plastic or on such materials as wood veneer, cloth, leather, or thin sheets of aluminum or steel! However, I would suggest you choose from among the many kinds of *paper* for your first greeting card—later, you might want to experiment with other materials.

The Grain of Paper

If you look at a wood strip in a hardwood floor, you'll see the long lines of the wood grain running the length of the strip, just as you can see the wood grain running the length of the boards in a table top. Similarly, paper has a grain running, generally, the length of the sheet. You can test this with a sheet of stock. Notice how much easier it is to fold the sheet from side to side—rather than from top to bottom. The paper resists less. Notice also that the crease is smooth rather than ragged. The grain runs from top to bottom, and you have folded with the grain. Folding from top to bottom, you would be working *against* the grain, and using more pressure to make a sharp crease. So try to fold *with* the grain of the paper when using a fold that folds only once or folds in the same direction several times.

You can quickly get the feel of the grain of paper by experimenting with accordion folds—multiple folds in the same direction—which we will discuss presently. You might not use a fold at all; a card of lightweight cardboard with an easel back (see Figures 6-7) might answer your needs. If you do this, have the grain of the easel running in the direction opposite to the grain of the card in order to provide a more rigid support.

What Kind of Fold to Use?

The whole idea of folding and unfolding your card is expansion; expansion and, in many cases, surprise. The way in which your cover design expands into the greeting depends largely on the way you fold your card. The fold is as

6. *To make an easel back, score a nearly triangular-shaped piece of cardboard, as shown here, bend the flap along the scoring, and paste it to the back of a card.*

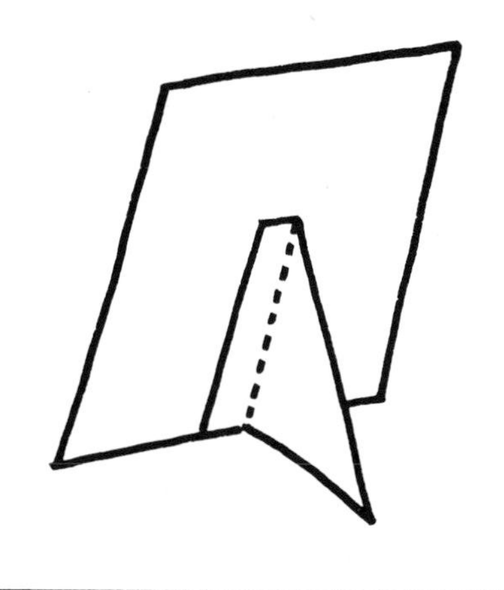

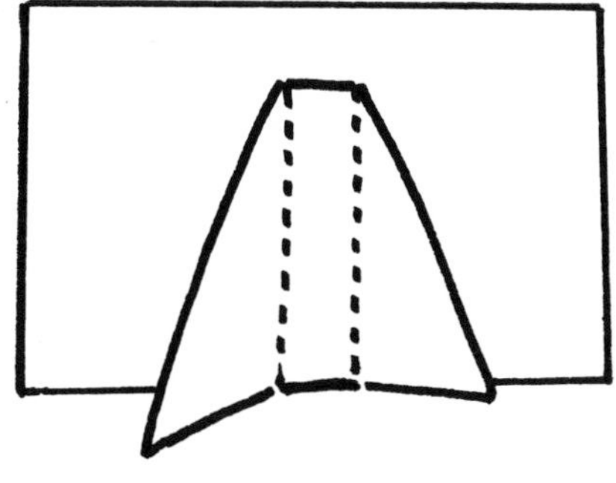

7. *Here is the rear view of two kinds of easel back cards.*

much a part of the design as the sketch itself. Don't neglect it.

First, there's a *simple fold.* This is a card which is folded over once, so that it forms a cover which is opened, revealing the message and signature inside. You can use a simple fold with a cartoon, opening to a gag line and your name. But you might want your card to expand in a way that is more lyrical, more imaginative. You just might want, let's face it, a card that suggests status, saying, "Look friend, a certain amount of my talent, time, and money went into preparing this little amusement for you!" This is why Valentines, for example, are generally elaborate. They suggest a great effort to please the recipient.

Folds can help you; they can expand with the insouciance of paper dolls, stand up with the dignity of an attache case, unfold with the grandeur of antique screens, or pop open like a jack-in-the-box. So whether your card will make use of a long, short, gate, box, or some other kind of fold will depend on the idea you'd want to express.

The Double or French Fold

One of the most widely used folds for greeting cards is the double, or French fold (see Figure 8). Double folds luxuriously suggest that you are using twice as much paper as you need. Actually, it is an economical fold, because you need to print only *one* side of the sheet: the design is drawn in one corner, the greeting in another (upside down)—and the paper is then folded like a table napkin. But since paper is stiffer than cloth, we can stand up our birthday greeting on a desk or dresser as if it were an open book.

If we place one French fold inside another and trim off the fold at the top, we have a sixteen page booklet which we can staple together or bind with cord for a greeting that might be a grouping of little pictures, an illustrated ballad, a reprinted essay, or whatever you desire.

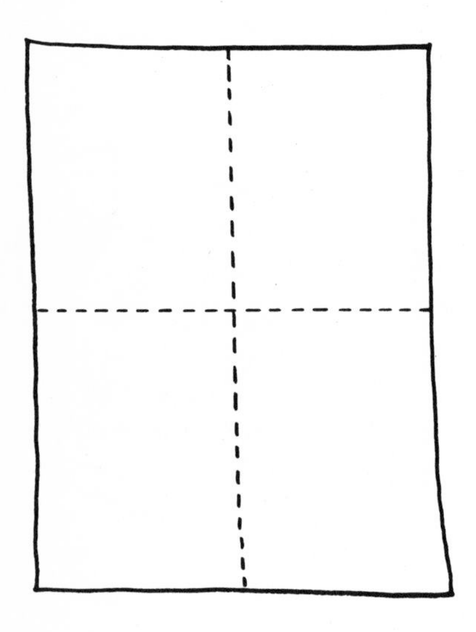

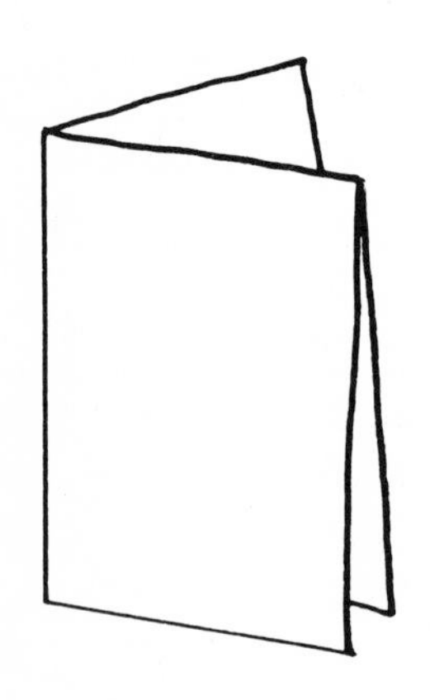

8. *Here is a French double fold.*

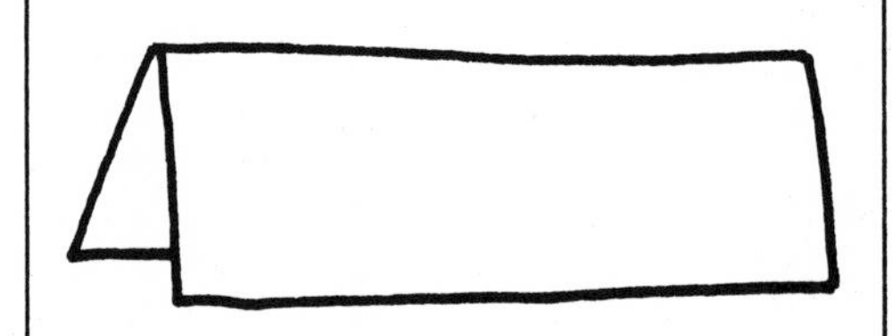

9. *Horizontal, long fold card.*

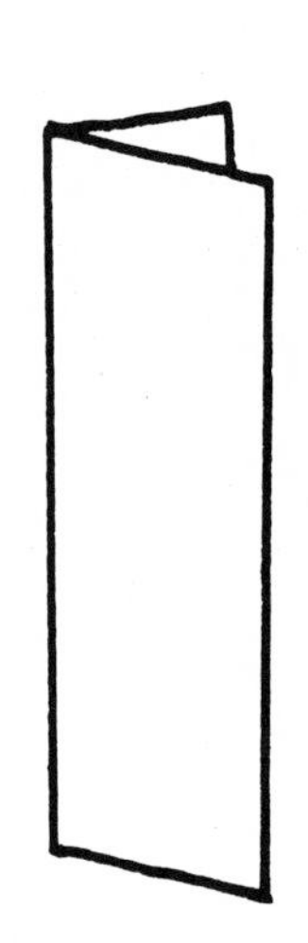

10. *Vertical, long fold card.*

Long and Short Folds

A long fold card is made by folding with the length of the card. If it's a vertical long fold, the fold is at the left hand side like a book. A horizontal long fold is folded at the top, like most calendars.

Similarly, a *short* fold card is folded along the short side of the card. For a vertical design, the fold would be at the top; for a horizontal design, at the left side. (See Figures 9-12.)

11. *Horizontal, short fold card.*

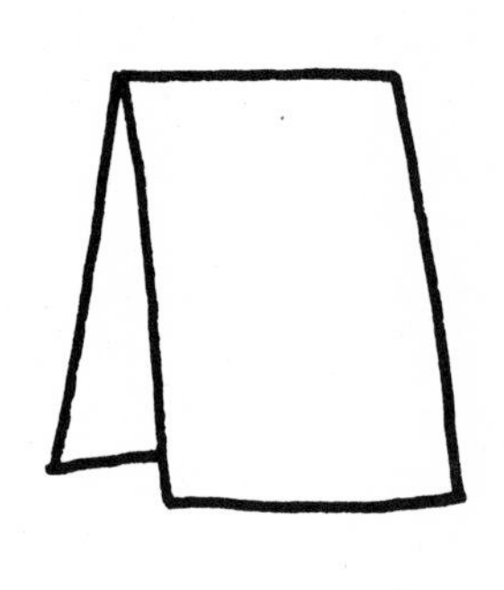

12. *Vertical, short fold card.*

Gate and Box Folds

A gate fold card is folded twice in the same direction, and opens like a screen to show three panels. (Figures 13-14.)

A box fold folds four times in the same direction to make two long sides and two short ends, plus an overlapping short end which is pasted to make a fold which will stand up like a box without a top or a bottom. (See Figures 15-16.) Cut-outs are often made in the face of box folds so that you can see through to the back like a stage setting. (See page 129 for directions in making a box fold.)

13. *Simple gate fold: folded twice in the same direction, it opens like a screen to show three panels.*

14. *Variation on the gate fold card.*

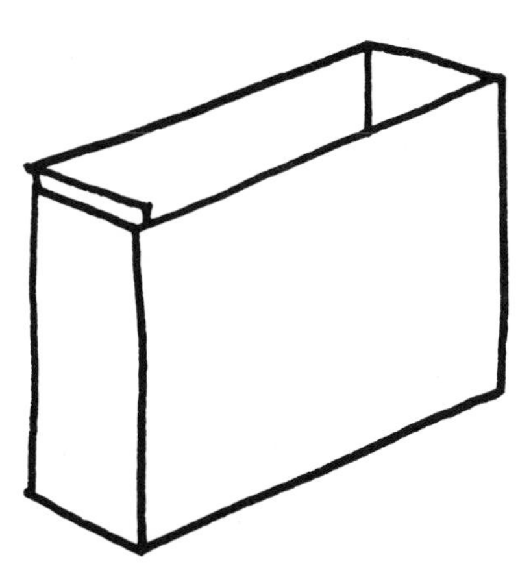

15. *Simple box fold: folds four times in the same direction to make two long sides, and two short ends—plus an overlapping short end which is pasted down. See also page 129.*

16. *Variations on the box fold card.*

Accordion and Pop-up Folds

An accordion fold is folded in alternate directions, with the grain, for as many folds as you like. Paper dolls are cut from this kind of fold. (Figures 17-18.)

The principle of the *reverse* fold is used in making pop-up cards. First make a French fold. Make a pencil dot on the inside of the center fold, one third of the distance down from the top (Figure 19). Now, grasp the top of the card with your left hand; with your right thumb and forefinger reverse the center fold from the pencil dot to the bottom of the card, forming a V shape. Crease (Figure 20). When you open the card, the V will pop out (Figure 21). Your print on the French fold, or on a cut-out print pasted over the fold, can suggest a bouquet, a nose, a jack-in-the-box, a fanciful animal, or whatever you think of.

Pop-up folds can also be cut from a simple fold of construction paper, using pairs of cuts of the same length of parallel, oblique, or curved lines. Pull the cut portions toward you, reversing the fold. Press down. These pop out when you open the card (Figure 22).

Pasted in cut-outs, using reverse folds, can be created for more elaborate pop-ups. (See Figure 23.)

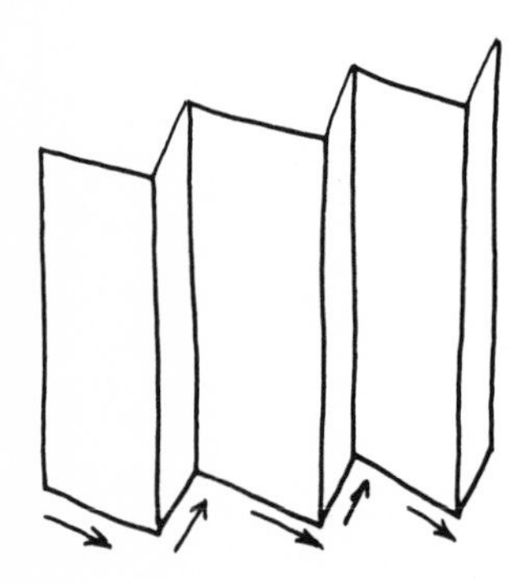

17. *Accordion fold: folds in alternate directions with the grain.*

18. *Paper dolls are cut from the same kind of accordion folds.*

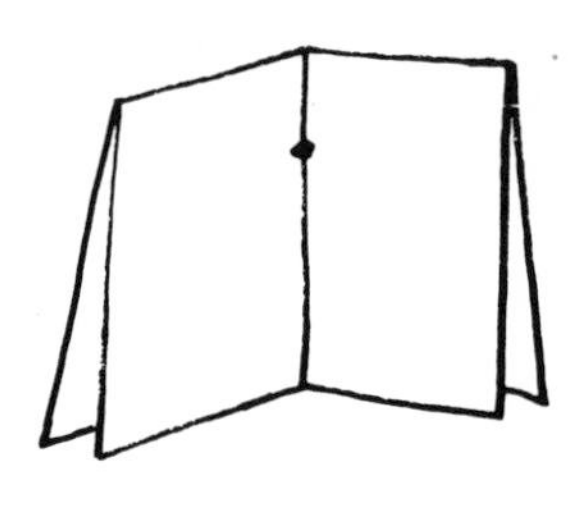

19. *Make a pencil dot on the inside of a French fold.*

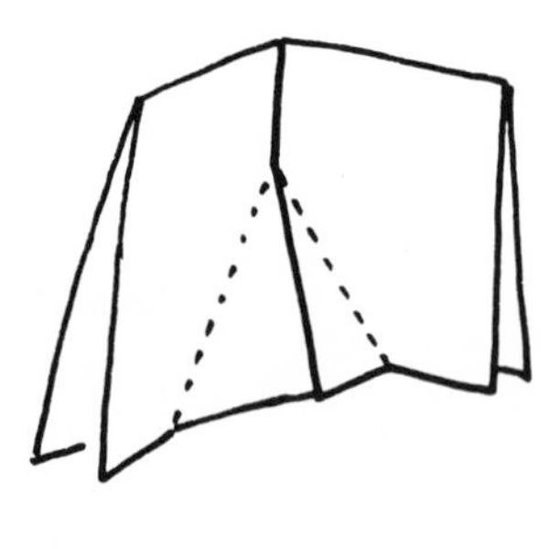

20. *Make a crease from the dot to the base of the fold.*

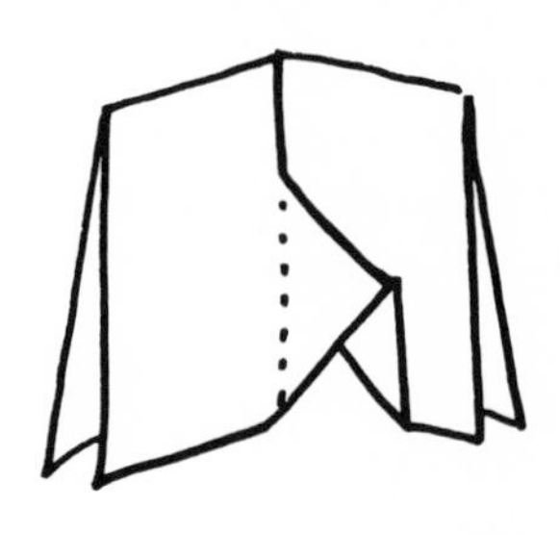

21. *When you open the card, the V shape will pop out.*

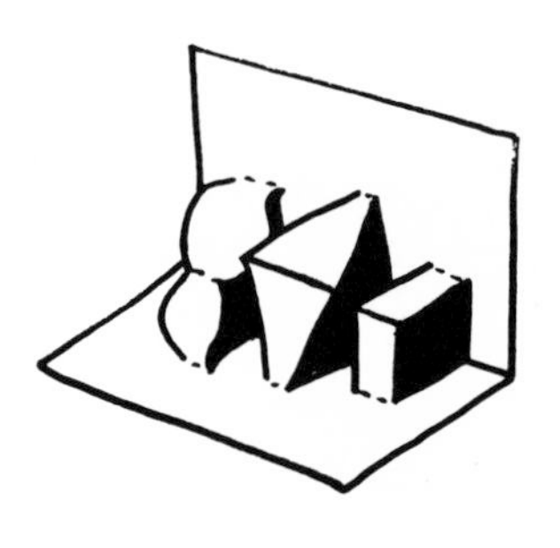

22. *Here is a pop-up fold using pairs of cuts of the same length of parallel, oblique, or curved lines.*

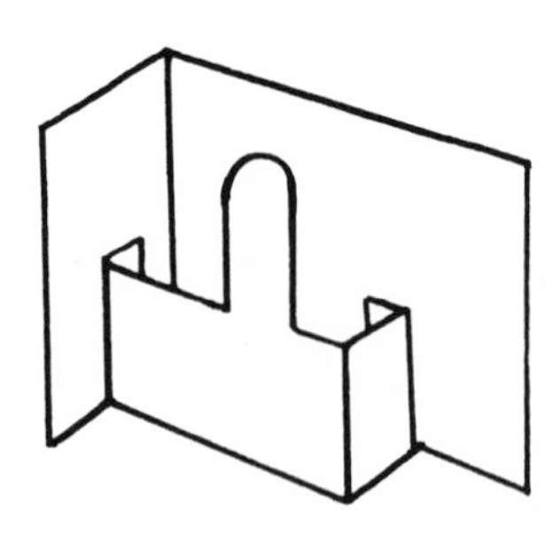

23. *Here is a pasted in cut-out which will pop up as the card is opened.*

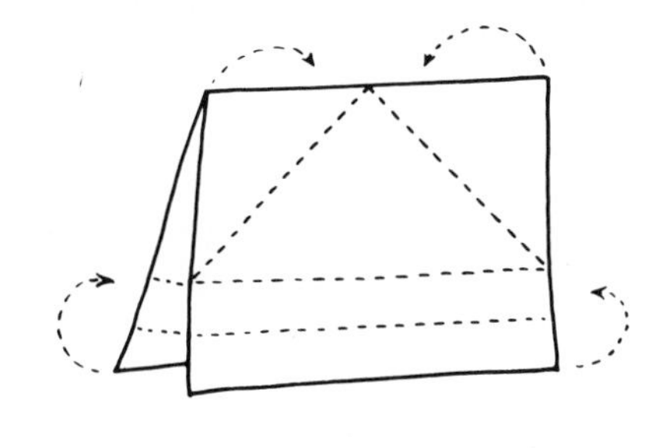

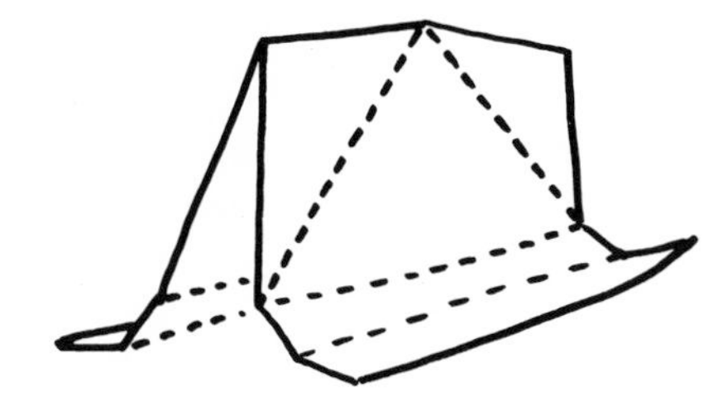

24. *Making the paper hat.*

Other Folds

Although paper stabiles and ornaments designed for hanging aren't folds in the greeting card sense, they are, nevertheless, collapsible, and can fit into envelopes as unusual cards. So study the diagram here for methods of making jointed and woven dolls (of paper) — using paper fasteners at the joints — paper hats, boats, and standing trees. Your own ingenuity can enlarge on these for a variety of effects. (See Figures 24-27.)

25. *A hanging card can be made from woven strips of paper.*

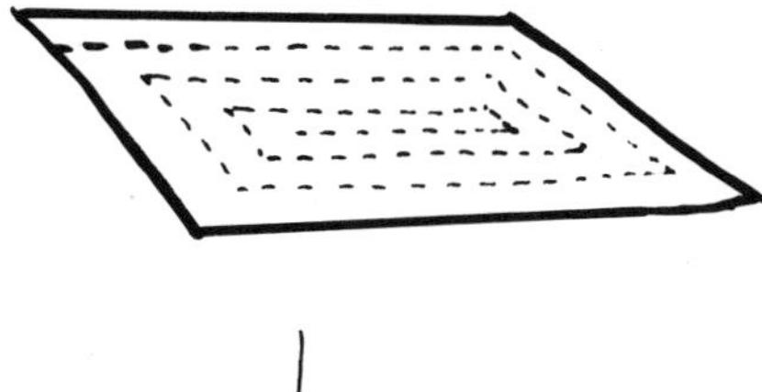

26. *By cutting a spiral-like design into a sheet of paper, you can unfold an attractive hanging ornament like this one.*

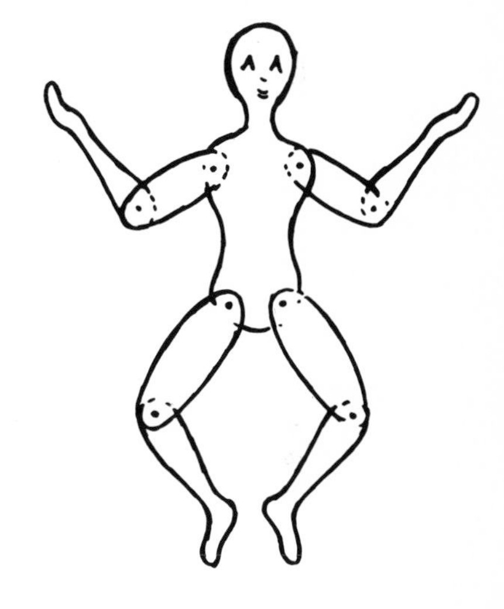

27. *Here is a diagram for a jointed figure which can be adapted for a greeting card. The joints are connected by paper fasteners. It will collapse and fold right into an envelope.*

Envelopes

Before designing and printing your cards, it's wise to have in mind (or better yet, on hand) the envelope you will use. Obviously, you won't want your card folded unattractively just to make it fit the "only envelopes they had in the store." Yes, envelopes can be made by hand, but first let's discuss the envelopes you can buy.

Ready-made envelopes come in a range of colors and textures at art supply stores. They generally come in standard, squarish sizes: 4⅜" x 5⅜", 5¼" x 7", 4¾" x 6½", 3⅜" x 8⅛", and even larger. With the larger size envelope, you'll need stiffeners to protect your card: you will need not one, but *two* stiffening cardboards to keep the delivery men from breaking the card as they force it into the narrow mail boxes. A long, narrow envelope (3¾" x 8⅛") comes in various colors available at art supply stores. The *smallest* size envelope accepted by the United States Post Office is 3" x 4¼", so your miniature cards must be sent in handmade envelopes placed inside larger ones.

Remembering that too *small* an envelope presents stamp canceling problems for the post office, and that too *large* an envelope presents delivery problems, you might want to concentrate on the two most convenient envelope sizes. These envelopes, available for pennies from every stationer and drug store are in standard sizes: 6¾" x 3⅝" made for a standard 8½" x 11" sheet folded first in half from top to bottom and then over in thirds from left to right; or the No. 10 envelope, which is designed for standard 8½" x 11" sheets folded in thirds from top to bottom; or the envelopes measuring 4⅛" x 9½". You can easily insert a larger card into these envelopes making a gate, accordion, or box fold.

You can also enhance these standard plain white envelopes with a stamp printed decorative band, or you can line them with colored or metallic paper. And sometimes stationers carry these standard sizes made out of mimeograph stock (for billings, etc.), tinted yellow, pink, or blue.

Making Your Own Envelope

If you want to send a card in an unusual envelope, you can easily make your own. This way, you can utilize imaginative papers and dimensions. Work from a pattern or from an envelope torn apart.

Envelopes are cut from the sheet diagonally (on the bias, if you sew) for greater strength, so carefully position your pattern of lightweight cardboard or stencil paper on the paper. Then lightly trace around the edges with a lead pencil and cut out the pattern with scissors (Figure 28). When you've cut out the envelope shape (Figure 29), lay it flat on a piece of cardboard. Then, using a brass-edged ruler and a table knife, score or crease the lines indicated in Figure 30. Tip on a decorative liner in your envelope (Figure 31). Now fold over the two side flaps (Figure 32), apply a thin strip of paste to the flaps, fold up the bottom flap, and press it down with your fingers (Figure 33). The top flap folds over and pastes down to seal in your greeting. You might want to seal your envelopes with sealing wax, pressing a linocut design into the wax. Gummed stars or red or gold notarial seals can dress up your envelopes, and you can also design and print seals drawn to represent owls, lions, faces, the sun, etc.

If you plan to use a bright, highly decorative paper for making your envelopes, design a plain sticker for an address label. This will provide maximum legibility in the post office; it's no good constructing a magnificent envelope that will arrive late, or not at all, simply because the pen lines of the address are vibrating in a sea of color, impossible to read!

If you have plenty of time, here's an amusing stunt you can do with hand-made envelopes: design and make a series of envelopes in successively smaller sizes, using contrasting colors, so that you end up with a tiny envelope containing a postage-stamp sized card. You'll get nothing but exclamations, *oh's* and *ah's* from the receivers as they remove the zebra-striped envelope from the polka dotted one, the envelope made from a paper printed with cabbage roses from the shiny black one!

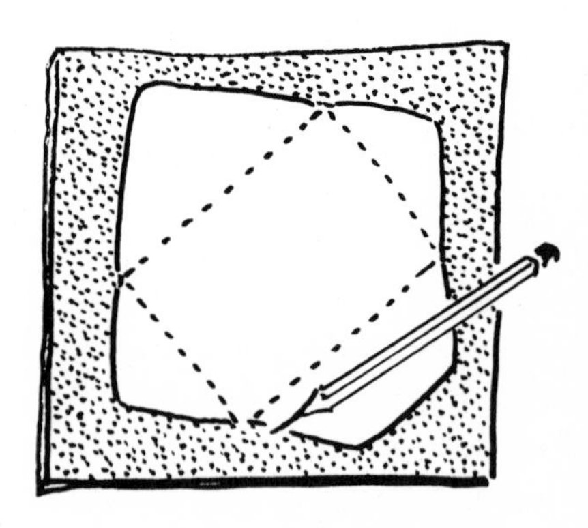

28. *With a pencil, trace around the edges of your pattern onto a heavy piece of paper.*

29. *Cut out the pattern with a scissors.*

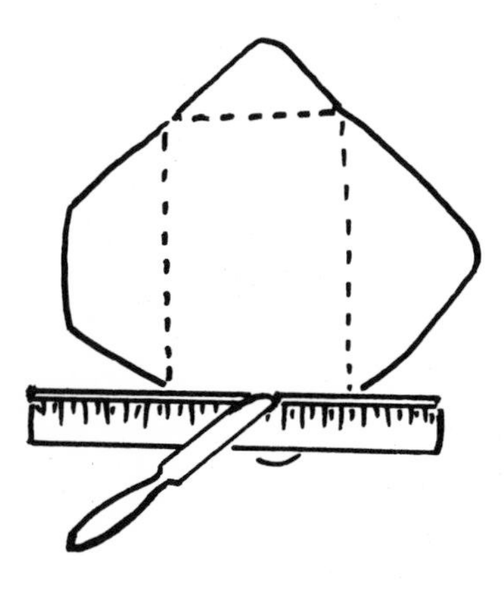

30. *With a table knife and ruler, score sheet of paper in the position indicated by the dotted lines.*

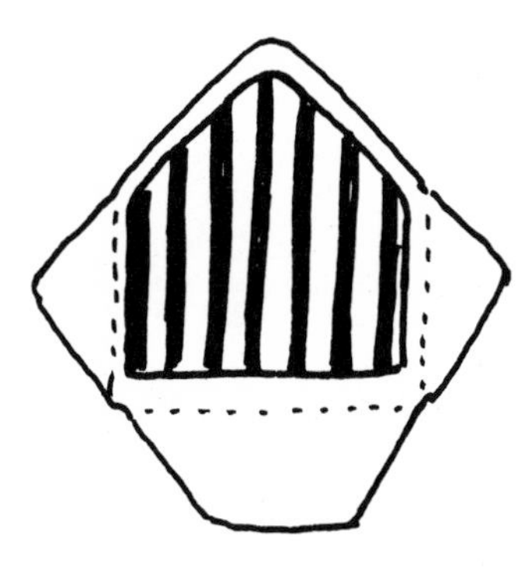

31. *Paste a decorative liner into your envelope.*

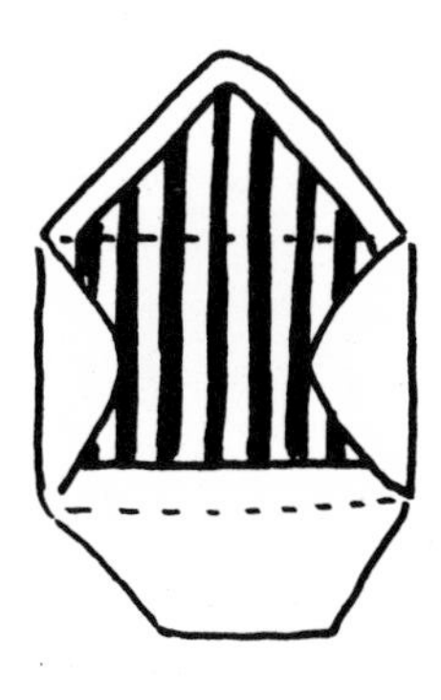

32. *Fold over the two side flaps.*

33. *Apply a thin strip of paste to the side flaps and fold up the bottom flap so that it adheres to the two side flaps.*

34. *You can make envelopes out of decorative paper. Add a plain sticker to the addressing area of the envelope.*

Self Mailers and Tubes

Perhaps you'd like to forget the envelopes althogether. Fold your card in half or in thirds, seal it with a notarial seal, or with one you have designed yourself, then address, stamp, and mail it. (Figure 35.)

A greeting designed as a broadside or poster might be as large as 18″ x 24″ or even bigger. Curvilinear or "psychedelic" bands of lettering, "art nouveau" patterns of figures and flowers, linoleum cuts, or tempera batiks big enough for framing, all can

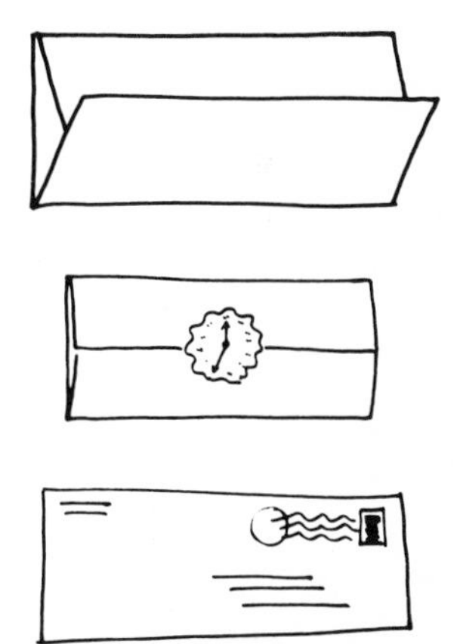

35. *To make a self mailer, simply fold the card in half or in thirds and seal it with a homemade seal. Address and send it off.*

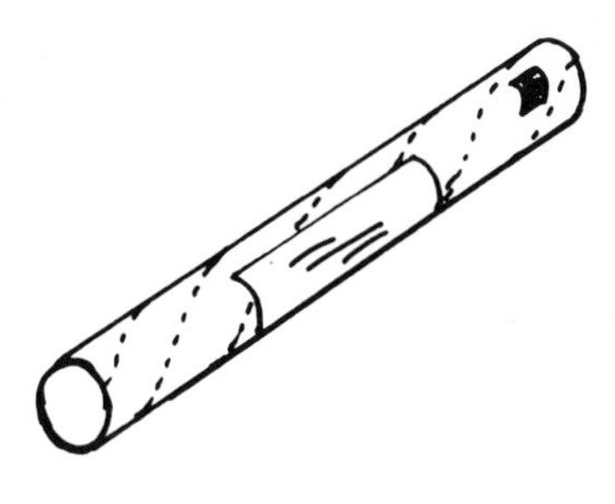

36. *Larger cards can be sent in a mailing tube.*

be mailed in cardboard tubes. (Figure 36.) Look in your classified telephone directory under *Paper Tubes* for the name of a supplier.

The mailing tube can be used as is, with a decorative mailing label, or it can be covered with a sheet of colored paper slightly wider than the length of the tube so that the ends can be tucked in. A *scroll* greeting card, unrolling to about 6″ x 30″, could be mailed in a tube 1″ in diameter and 7″ long and it will still fit in a mail box. A "parchment" paper wrap, impressively held with sealing wax, could add to the attractiveness of packaging such a greeting, especially if the address is written in calligraphic style with a broad nibbed pen.

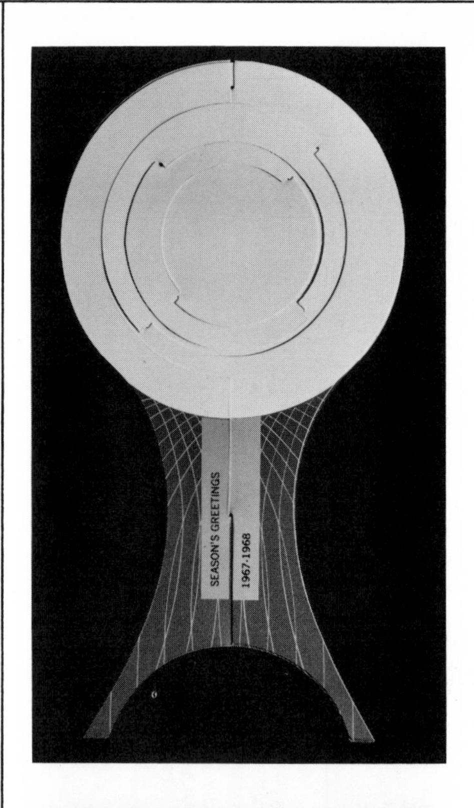

This three dimensional globe lies flat when unopened. It actually consists of two interlocking pieces of cardboard.

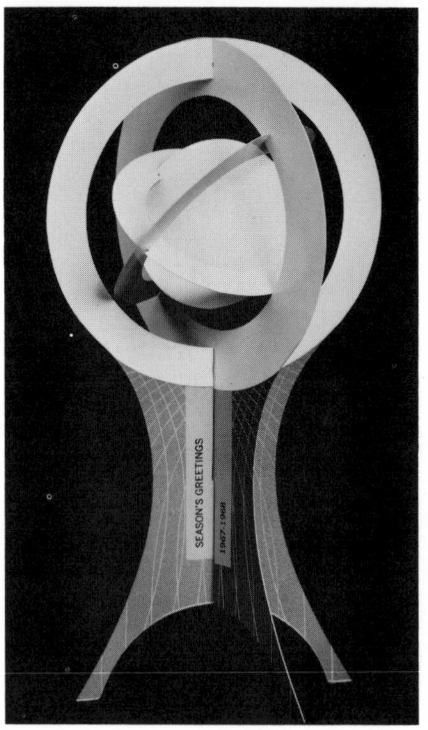

When opened, the card forms five interlocking circles. By Seymour Robins.

This card is constructed with pieces of felt pasted onto a textured wallpaper. The wallpaper has been mounted on a piece of card stock. By Margaret Rea.

Although commercially printed, this card may offer an interesting folding idea for you. Hoedt Studios.

This is a very delicately made Japanese Christmas card. A kite has been constructed with thin rice paper pasted onto fragile sticks. The kite is mounted inside the card. Bijutsu Shuppan-Sha.

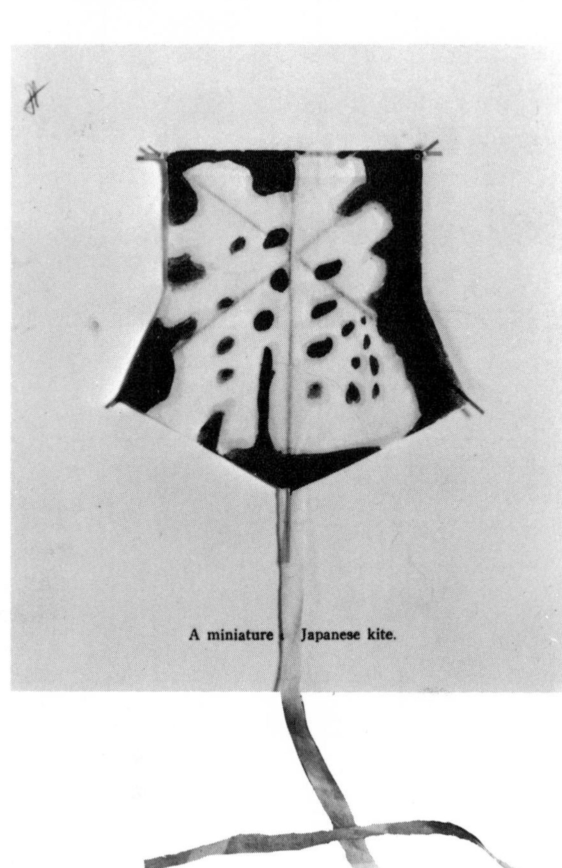

The face of this card is bright green. The artist has cut out panels in a spiral direction, pulled out and folded back the panels. The white paper from the inside makes a strong contrast. Leslie and Mort Junger.

This sunburst effect was produced by pulling back the folds of the card. An offset tracing has been mounted inside the fold. By John Carlis.

3

Offset Tracings

If you happen to have a piece of tracing paper on hand, you can make a few offset tracings within the next half hour. An offset tracing is nothing more than an image — say a leaf or a figure — seen through translucent paper and traced with a soft lead pencil. The soft lead pencil line is then turned face down on another sheet of paper, and rubbed briskly on the back with the bowl of a spoon. A half dozen copies can be offset onto cards very quickly in this way, and the subdued quality of the transferred line can be contrasted with touches of hand color.

Interesting atmospheric effects can be achieved with offset tracings: a mountain view, tug boats in a harbor, or a wooded path at dusk. That window box of geraniums you sketched at a friend's summer cottage, the museum postcard of a Renaissance candlestick in your files, or the magazine clipping you've saved of an arabesque ceramic tile, might be just what you need in developing a design.

A tracing will help if you want to reverse the direction of your drawing. It's also an ideal method for transferring a formal design from some printed source to your card. Coats of arms immediately come to mind, as well as amusing variations of heraldry, all of which are suitable for greetings.

Materials for Tracing

Pads of tracing paper in various sizes and weights, stocked in every art supply store.
Soft lead pencils: Eberhard Faber Ebony, Jet Black Extra Smooth #6325
Art gum eraser (for corrections or changes)
Tablespoon
Pastels
Colored pencils
Colored felt tip marking pens
Colored inks, pens, and small camel hair brushes
X-Acto knife
Metallic foils
Fixative or clear plastic spray
Cellophane or frisket tape
Sequins; flat-backed rhinestones

Rubbing Down

After you've made your sketch or selected a printed piece of art, place the tracing paper over the art, securing the corners with pieces of cellophane or frisket tape (Figure 37). (Frisket tape — a heavier weight, pressure sensitive tape — is somewhat easier to lift off than cellophane tape.) With a sharpened, soft pencil, proceed to outline the image you see through the tracing paper (Figure 38). (If you're tracing a valuable print, use a felt tipped or Pentel pen that will not mark the original with any indentations.)

Then, remove the sketch and turn over the tracing paper. Work on the *back* of the tracing paper with a soft lead pencil, carefully going over the lines that show through (Figure 39). Work on a smooth, hard surface to be sure you get a good, heavy line of graphite.

Now turn over the tracing paper and place your card underneath the sheet so that the graphite side is in contact with the card. Briskly rub the tracing paper with the bowl of a tablespoon (Figure 40). The lines of the drawing will transfer to the card. A little practice will show you how to rub down a clean line quickly, and you should be able to get six or eight impressions before the graphite on the back of the tracing

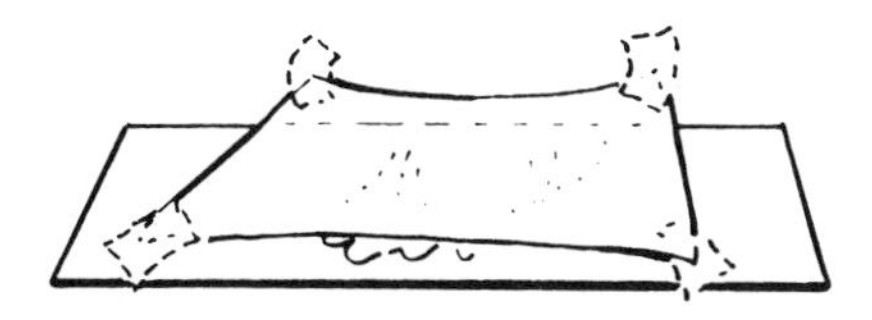

37. Secure the four corners of the tracing paper over the art, using cellophane or frisket tape.

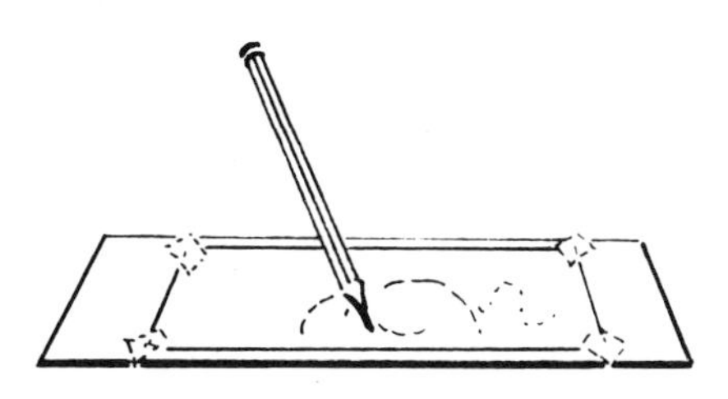

38. Trace the image over the tracing

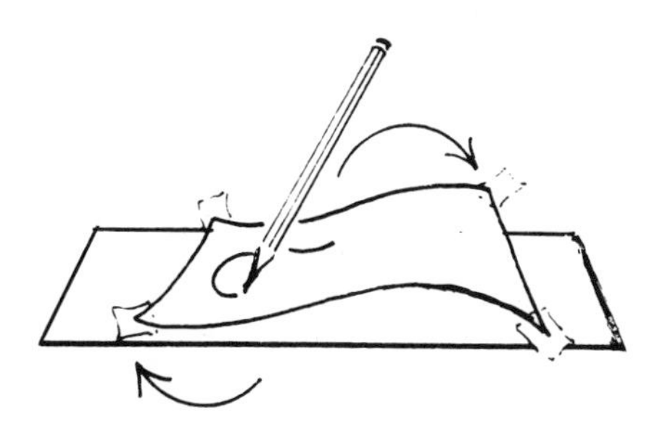

39. Remove the sketch; turn over the tracing paper; go over the lines with a soft lead pencil.

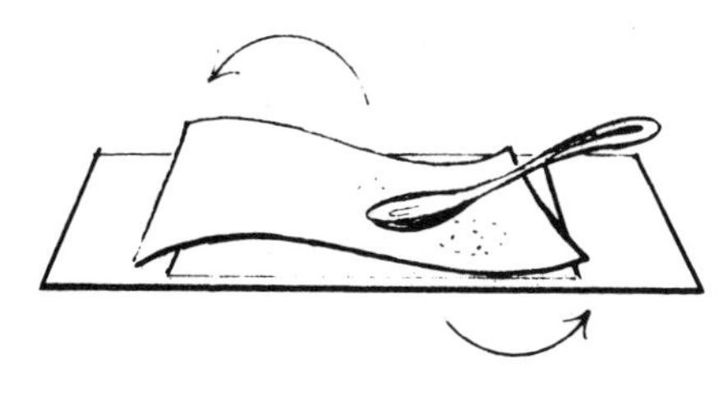

40. Put the blank card under the tracing paper, soft pencil line in contact with the card, and rub tracing paper with the bowl of a spoon.

sheet is used up. When you can no longer get any impressions from the sheet, add another soft pencil line on the back of the tracing.

Decorating

Spread your six or eight impressions in front of you on your work table, and add color (Figure 41). You can color with just about anything: colored pencils, pastels, Pentel pens, brush and colored inks, or watercolor. If you use pastels, spray lightly with plastic spray or with fixative. Add any lettering with a felt tipped pen. Perhaps you'll want to tip on (paste) a brilliantly colored rhinestone onto the card, or paste the design onto a contrasting folder.

Translucent Effects

Fold a piece of 7″ x 10″ heavy tracing paper in half, lengthwise. Then fold the sheet in half again, making a French fold, 3½″ x 5″, as shown in Figure 42. On the face of this fold, rub down a tracing and hand color a design. If you use pastels, spray with fixative or clear plastic spray.

Now, opening the card halfway (to 3½″ x 10″) and placing it against a sheet of cardboard, cut out a small portion of the design with your X-Acto knife (Figure 43). Cut a piece of metallic paper just a little bit smaller than 3½″ x 10″. Now refold your book fold to 3½″ x 5″, insert and paste the gold or silver paper beneath your design. (See Figure 44.)

Since the heaviest tracing paper is like vellum, your design will have an over-all faint glimmer of gold or silver, except for the portion you cut out, which will shine brightly.

41. Add color to offset tracings.

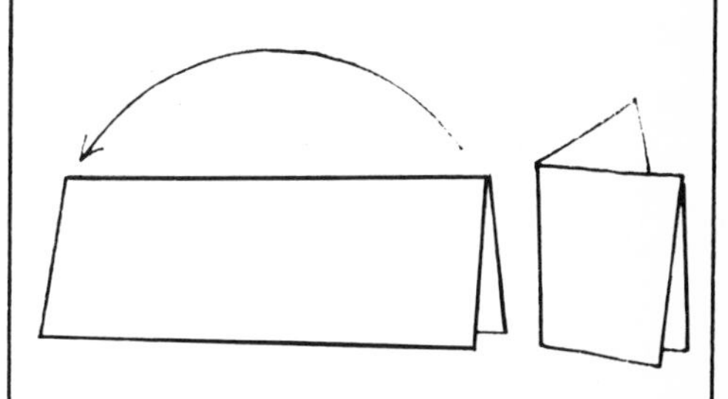

42. Make a French fold with heavy tracing paper.

43. After rubbing down a design on the face of the card, cut out portions of the design with X-Acto knife.

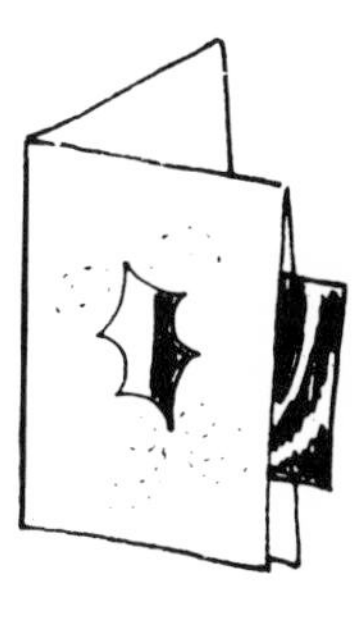

44. Insert metallic paper beneath the design.

Bisymmetric and Quartered Patterns

Fold medium weight tracing paper in half, and draw a design on the top half. Turn the fold over, and trace the design on the other half of the paper (Figure 46). Graphite side down, and using the bowl of a spoon, rub down the design onto the other fold (Figure 47). If you're going to use two figures duplicated on each side, equidistant from the center, this method will ensure symmetry.

To make a symmetrical floral design, fold your medium weight tracing paper in quarters, drawing a design on the top quarter. Trace this pattern onto the remaining three quarters. Rub down the design. When you open up the fold, you will have a symmetrical design (Figure 48). Try the same idea by folding the paper in eighths. You will find this procedure of folding, tracing, and rubbing a great time saver for reproducing many patterns. It's ideal for borders, within which you can place various motifs.

45. *Fold medium weight tracing paper in half, and draw a design on the top half of the paper.*

46. *Turn the fold over and trace the design on the other half of the paper.*

47. *Rub down the design, open up the fold, and you will have two figures duplicated on each side.*

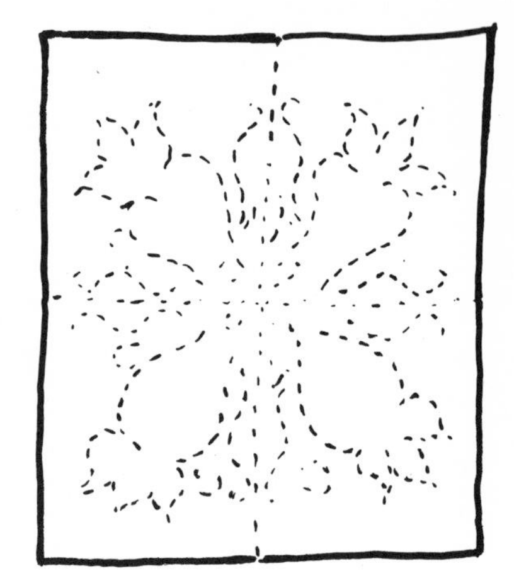

48. *By folding your paper in quarters, and tracing the design, you can reproduce a full, symmetrical floral pattern as shown here.*

This is an offset tracing of a 15th century woodcut illustration of Sagittarius. The tracing was made on pale yellow bond, mounted on a square of bright orange gift wrapping, again mounted on Japanese rice paper. By John Carlis.

This offset tracing was mounted on red card stock. With a red felt tip pen, touches of color were added in the holly, on the cat's whiskers, and on the stamps. By John Carlis.

This pop art card was produced by transferring newspaper illustrations to bond paper with lighter fluid. Touches of color were added with felt-tip pens. The card was mailed in a paper tube.

4

Rubbings

In making tracings, you learned how friction could help you create greeting cards, because you discovered that you could turn a sketch face down on a fresh sheet of paper, *rub* the back of the drawing, and get several copies of the original sketch in reverse. You'll now use friction in another way, by making a friction print called a *rubbing*.

A rubbing is the kind of print made when a crayon or pencil is passed over the surface of paper which is pressed against a relief surface, the higher portions picking up the ink, pencil, or crayon, and thus indicating the pattern. When we were children, we all made rubbings of coins by rubbing a crayon over a paper which was laid over the coin. An interesting characteristic of rubbings is that the drawing implement never touches the actual printing surface; the printing surface remains clean. Using old book bindings, embossed lids of antique boxes, embossed table mats, or even old buttons, rubbings can become greeting cards, with probably less effort than making any of the other cards suggested in this book.

First, let's start by making a rubbing with found objects.

Materials for Rubbing Found Objects

Old book bindings; coins; tooled leather desk sets; tooled leather handbags; cowboy belts; relief tiles; table mats; carved box tops, etc.
Soft lead pencils
White and colored crayon pencils
Wax crayons
Scissors
Sheets of colored paper and odds-and-ends of gift wrapping
Brass-edged ruler
X-Acto knife or single-edged razor blade
Elmer's Glue-All
Fixative or clear plastic spray

Rubbing Found Objects

Somewhere on your bookshelves, you may be able to find a nineteenth century geography book that hasn't been tossed out, or an old cookbook or photo album with some interesting embossing on the cover.

Place a sheet of typewriter paper over the raised design and, with a soft lead colored pencil, or a crayon, using an even pressure, quickly rub from left to right. Still holding the paper in position, rub the other way at a right angle to your first lines (Figures 50-51).

49. *Find a book with an embossed cover for your design motif.*

Trimming

Use your brass-edged ruler as a guide to trim away the unwanted portions of the rubbing with an X-Acto knife or a single-edged razor blade (Figure 52).

Rubbings from Your Own Reliefs

Now why not try a rubbing made from one of your *own* carved reliefs? There are four kinds of carved relief surfaces: (1) linoleum cut; (2) carved plaster; (3) modeled and carved self-hardening clay; (4) built-up acrylic base. Let's take them in that order: first, the linoleum cut. Then we'll proceed with the others.

Materials for a Linoleum Cut Rubbing

Set of Speedball linoleum cutting tools
Linoleum
Sheets of thin, strong paper
Watercolor brushes, nos. 7 and 9
Saucer of water
Clean cloth
Inking wad, made from rags tied tightly together by a clean cloth
Tube of printer's ink: black or terracotta
Blotters
Piece of glass (about 9" x 12")

Cutting the Linoleum

Transfer your design (Figure 53) to the surface of the linoleum with an offset tracing (see Chapter 3). Then make a shallow cut around the outline of your design with the smallest V-cut lino-cutting tool (Figure 54). Cut against this first cutting line with a U-shaped cutter, finally cutting to a depth of about ⅜". Brush out any bits of linoleum with a large watercolor brush.

50. *Place a sheet of typewriter paper over the raised design.*

51. *With a pencil or crayon, rub quickly from left to right; then up and down.*

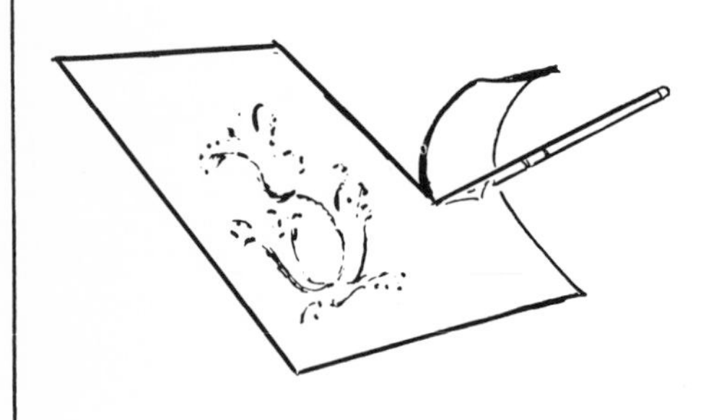

52. *Trim away unwanted portions.*

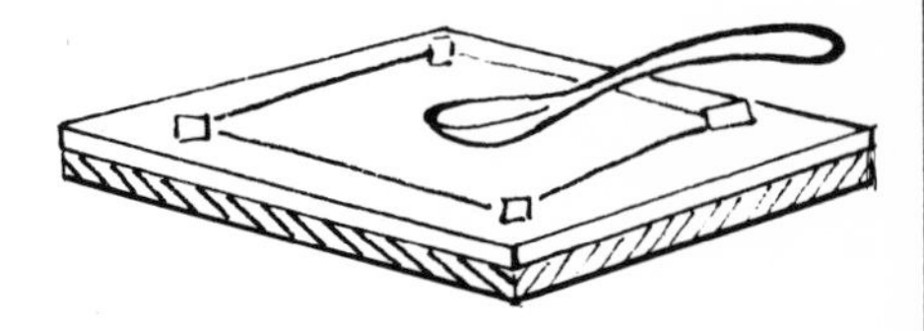

53. *Make an offset tracing on the linoleum surface.*

54. *With your smallest V-cut lino-cutting tool, make a shallow outline of your design; then go over the cut with a U-shaped cutter.*

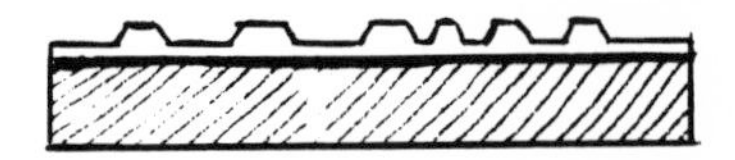

55. *Cross section of the cut linoleum block: depth of cut is about ⅜".*

56. *Pass a wet brush back and forth over the printing paper.*

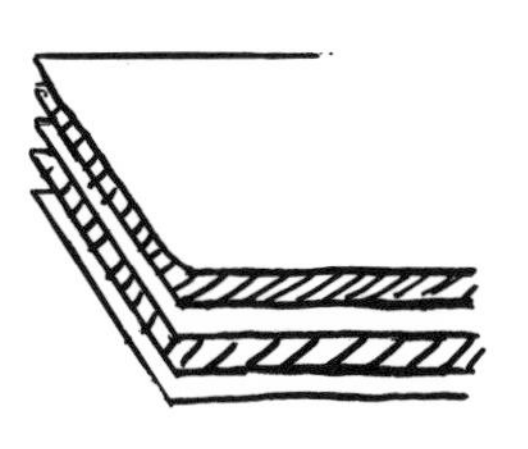

57. *Sandwich the damp sheets of paper between blotters.*

Dampening the Paper

Dip a large watercolor brush into a saucer of water and pass the wet brush quickly back and forth over the paper (Figure 56). Place the paper between blotters, and then dampen another sheet, building up a sandwich of dampened paper and blotters (Figure 57). Let them stand for several hours, so that the paper will not be wet, but just damp enough so that it can be pressed into the valleys of the linoleum cut.

Printing from the Linoleum Cut

Dab some printer's ink onto the piece of glass with a wad of rags tied tightly into a clean cloth, a bundle which will act as an inker (see Figure 58). Next, place a sheet of the dampened paper over the cut linoleum and, with a clean cloth, gently press down the paper into all of the valleys. Care must be taken not to tear the paper. When the paper is all worked down, pick up some ink with the inking wad by dabbing the wad on the inked glass (Figure 60). Now dab the surface of the paper. The paper should have been worked far enough down so that only the top surface will receive ink. After the inking, allow a minute or so for the paper to dry, then carefully lift it away from the linocut (Figure 61).

Now let's try a rubbing from a carved plaster surface.

58. *Dab printer's ink onto a piece of glass, using a bundle of rags as a dabber.*

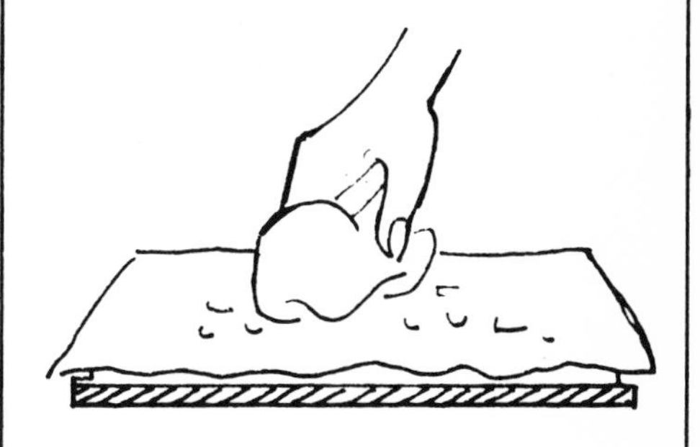

59. *Gently press dampened paper over the cut linoleum. Be sure to work paper into the valleys of cuts on the linoleum.*

60. *Press inked dabber onto the surface of the paper.*

61. *Lift the paper from the linocut.*

Materials for a Plaster Surface Rubbing

Box top (about 10″ x 15″, ½″ deep)
Set of Speedball linoleum cutting tools
Box of casting plaster
Sheets of thin, strong paper
Watercolor brushes
Saucer of water
Clean cloth
Inking wad of cloths tied tightly together by a clean cloth
Tube of printer's ink: black or terracotta
Blotters
Piece of glass (about 9″ x 12″)

Preparing the Plaster

Pour some plaster of Paris into a box top, about 10″ x 15″, and ½″ deep (Figure 62). Let the plaster set, and just before it's bone dry, tear off the box paper from the bottom (Figure 63). Roll off any remaining bits of damp paper with your finger or with a cloth to prepare this flat surface for your sketch.

Transfer your design (Figure 64) to the surface of the plaster with an offset tracing (see Chapter 3). You might want to reinforce the offset tracing with a soft pencil line.

Now cut around the outline of your design with the smallest V-cut linocutting tool (Figure 65). Dip a watercolor brush into the saucer of water and wet the line you've just cut (Figure 66). Then cut against this first cutting line with a U-shaped cutter, finally cutting to a depth of about ⅜″ (Figure 67). Brushing water onto the plaster from time to time will make the cutting easier. When you've finished, brush out any remaining bits of plaster, and set the plaster relief aside to dry.

Now print from the plaster the way you printed from the linoleum cut.

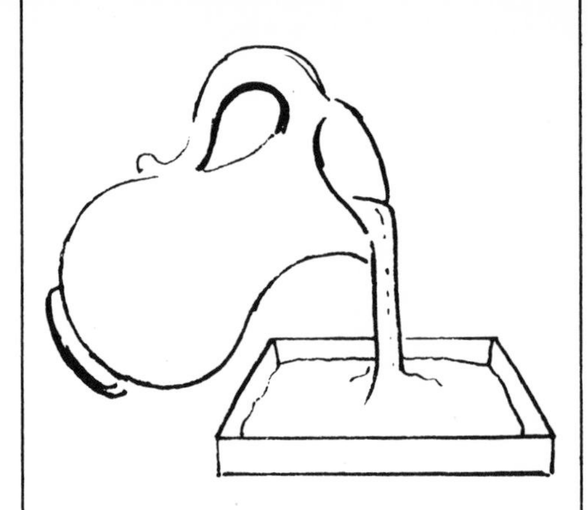

62. *Pour some plaster of Paris into a box top.*

63. *After the plaster has set, tear off damp box paper from the bottom.*

64. *Transfer design to plaster surface with an offset tracing.*

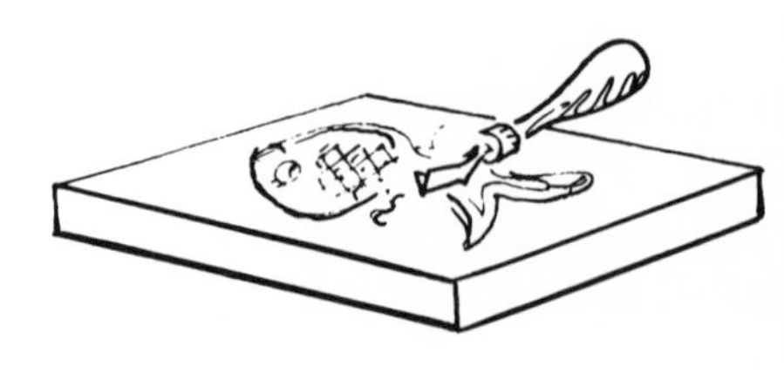

65. *Into the plaster, cut the outline of the design with your smallest V-cut linocutting tool.*

66. *Wet the cut outline with a watercolor brush, to make the additional cutting easier.*

67. *Using the U-shaped cutter, make a deeper cut into the outline, to a depth of about ⅜″.*

Materials for Clay Surface Rubbings

Box of Stewart's self-hardening modeling clay
Clay modeling tools
Set of Speedball linoleum cutting tools
Bottle
Sheets of thin, strong paper
Watercolor brushes
Saucer of water
Clean cloth
Inking wad of cloths tied tightly by a clean cloth
Tube of printer's ink: black or terracotta
Blotters
Piece of glass (about 9″ x 12″)

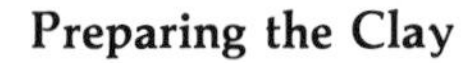

Preparing the Clay

Using a bottle as if it were a bread roller, roll out some Stewart's clay about ½″ in thickness, to an area of about 8″ x 10″. This will be your clay slab. Trim it to the size you want your cards (Figures 68-69). Pat this flat. Take another piece of clay and make some clay coils. Make a direct pattern on the clay slab with the coils (Figure 70).

Use clay modeling tools to modify and refine the design of the coils. Add some incised detail with linocutting tools (Figure 71). Let it dry.

Print from the clay in the same way you printed from the linoleum cut.

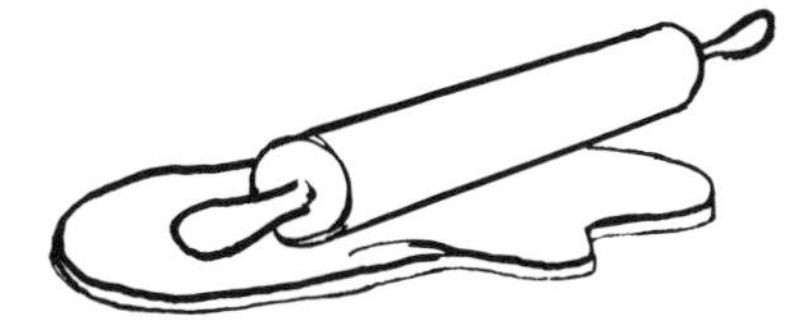

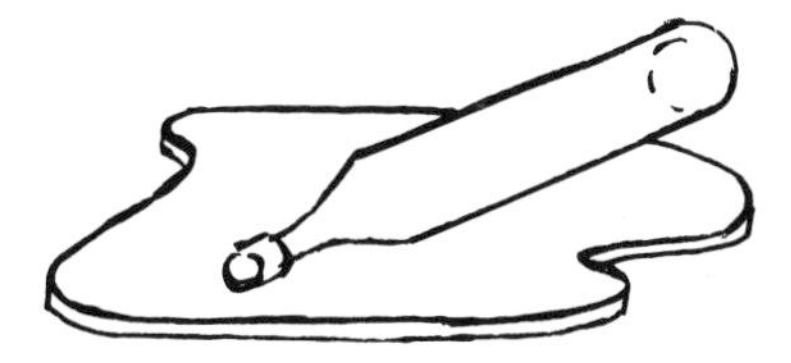

68. *Using a rolling pin or a bottle, flatten out some clay.*

69. *Trim the clay slab to the size you want your card to be.*

70. *Make a design on the clay slab with coils of clay.*

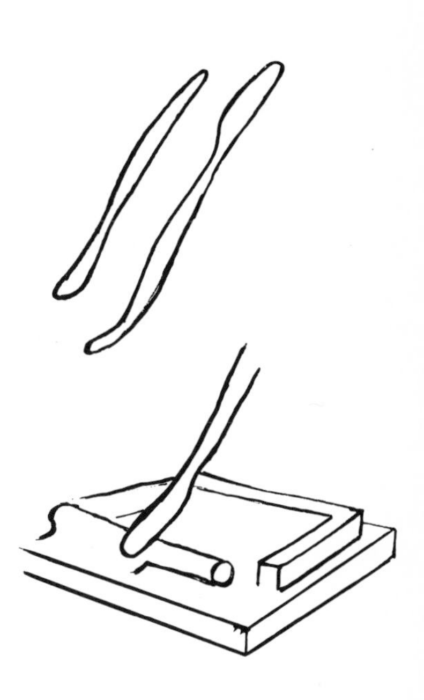

71. *Modify and refine the design with modeling tools.*

Materials for Acrylic Base Rubbings

Acrylic paint or modeling paste
Cardboard
Set of Speedball linoleum cutting tools
Sheets of thin, strong paper
Watercolor brushes
Saucer of water
Clean Cloth
Inking wad of cloths tied tightly together by a clean cloth
Tube of printer's ink: black or terracotta
Blotters
Piece of glass (about 9″ x 12″)

Preparing the Acrylic Surface

Sketch or offset a design on a piece of heavy cardboard. Paint onto the surface of the cardboard, using the acrylic paint (Figure 72). Let the paint dry, then build up the design in relief. Cut into the surface with linocutting tools (Figure 73). Build up other portions with more acrylic base; let it dry and carve again with linocutting tools. Repeat this until you're satisfied with your relief. (Acrylic modeling paste handles more like clay; it can be spooned on and spread around with bristle brushes or even ice cream sticks to build up a relief pattern.)

Follow directions for printing as described in printing from the linoleum block.

72. *Paint the cardboard, using acrylic paint or modeling paste.*

73. *Cut into the surface of the dried acrylic with linocutting tools.*

74. *Apply additional acrylic.*

75. *Again, carve into the acrylic with your linocutting tool.*

Large Rubbings

After experimenting with smaller sizes, you'll probably want to make rubbings up to 12″ x 18″. These are as easy to make as smaller rubbings and they make most impressive greetings. It's best to send them in a cardboard mailing tube.

Variations

Why not mount your rubbing? Select a paper of card weight in a color contrasting to the paper on which you did the rubbing. Make a book fold, and trim the card to the proper size. Put little dots of Elmer's glue on the back of the rubbing and tip (paste) it to the folder. Letter your greeting inside with a felt tipped pen. (See Figures 76-79.)

Try it another way: make a stand-up (box) fold for your rubbing, overlapping and pasting the end of the fold as shown in Figure 80.

You can also combine touches of hand coloring or a simple sketch with your rubbing. The *bon voyage* card shown in the illustration on page 46 was made with a rubbing of the center medallion of a book binding for the sun, with the addition of a little drawing for the face, mountains, and waves.

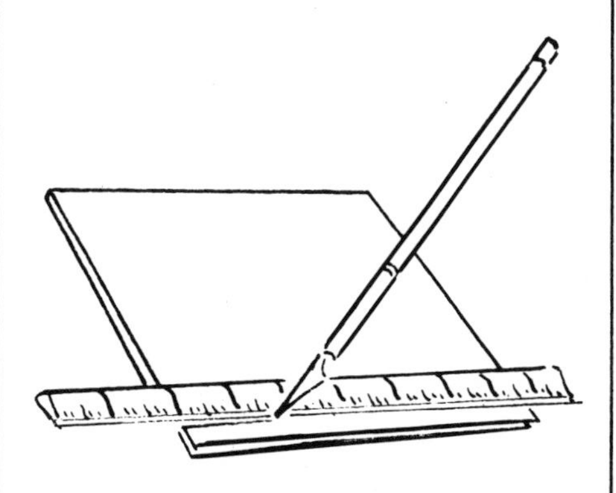

76. *Make a book fold and trim to desired size.*

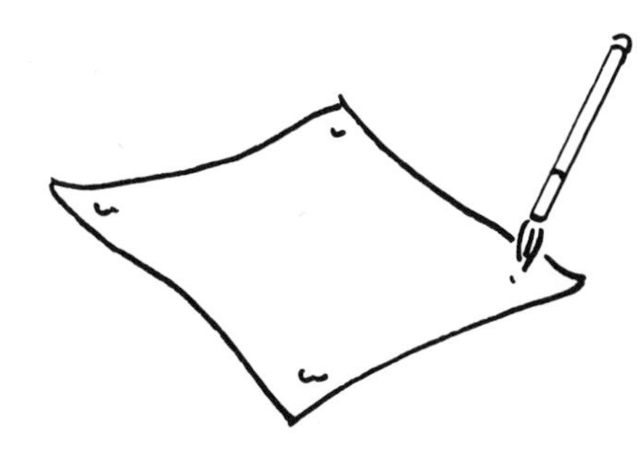

77. *Put four dots of glue on the back.*

78. *Paste the rubbing on the face of the book fold.*

79. *Letter your greeting inside.*

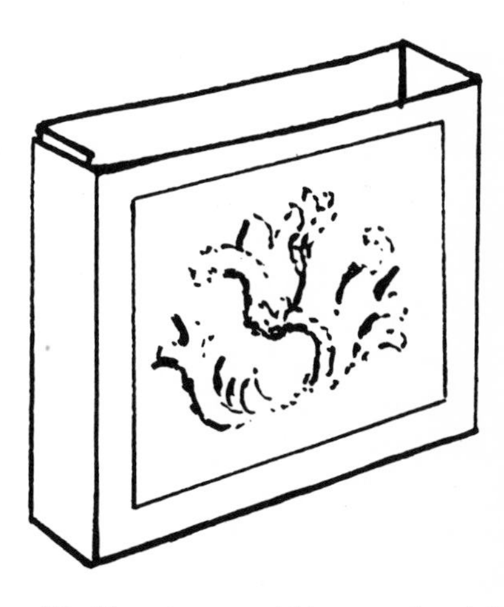

80. *Mount your rubbing on a box fold.*

Elaborate sunburst designs can be obtained by rubbing the embossing of old leather bound books. You can paste the rubbing on the card and draw around it as shown here. By John Carlis.

Here the artist placed pieces of cardboard and string under rice paper and rolled over the surface with a lightly charged brayer. She trimmed the paper and mounted it on card stock. By Margaret Rea.

This rubbing of a lion was mounted on cardboard, then mounted again on gift wrapping paper, and decorated with gold foil borders. By John Carlis.

You can buy old decorative wood blocks — once used for fabric printing and often available in antique stores — to make attractive rubbings. Like this one in three colors. By Renata Rainer.

5

Blot Prints

The dexterity you have acquired in making clean tracings and rubbings should now come to your aid in creating the most elementary kind of stamped print: the blot. This is the same principle as the reversed mirror image of your signature, the pattern seen on a fresh blotter. To make a blot print, you simply make a reverse image of a brush and ink sketch. Blotting from a hinged master sketch onto pristine sheets of fresh paper is an ancient and highly sophisticated Japanese graphic technique. With practice, this long forgotten method can produce skillful prints which will have the appearance of original ink sketches.

Line drawings made with small brushes in black waterproof ink lend themselves best to blot prints. You can add touches of watercolor to the finished prints if you like. Since little more than brush, ink, and paper is needed, the method is highly economical. I think you'll enjoy doing blot prints, too!

Materials for Blot Prints

Sketch pad and tracing paper
Pen, pencils
Eraser
Ruler
Small watercolor brush and black India ink
9″ x 12″ heavy board (or larger) or cardboard or ¼″ Masonite
4″ x 5″ cards
Role of 1″ or 1½″ wide frisket or masking tape
Sheet of celluloid or clear plastic medium weight
Talcum powder
Elmer's Glue-All
Clean cloth

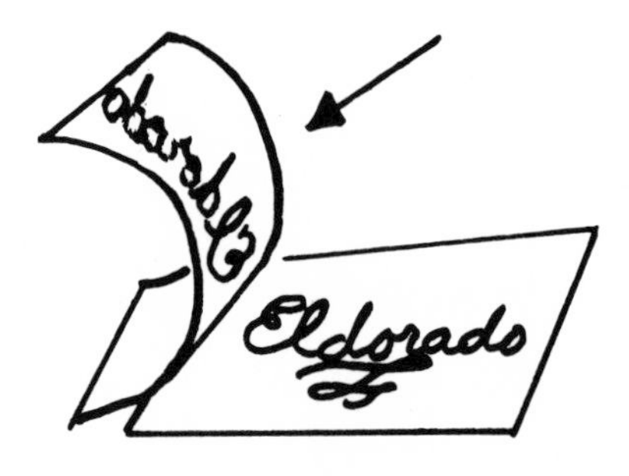

81. *Blot prints are based on the same principle as ink blotters.*

Preparing the Hinged Board

Place the 9″ x 12″ heavy cardboard or Masonite on your work table in a horizontal position in front of you. With the ruler and pencil, mark a center line on the board, giving you a left and right hand area of 6″ x 9″ (Figure 82). Place the 5″ side of a 4″ x 5″ piece of heavy celluloid or .00 weight clear plastic acetate alongside the center line, 2″ from the top, bottom, and right hand edges of the board (Figure 83).

Fasten the plastic to the board with a 5″ strip of 1″ masking tape, ½″ fastened down to the board, the other ½″ fastened to the clear acetate as shown in Figure 84.

Flop the acetate to the left hand side of the board, and reinforce the hinge with another 5″ strip of 1″ masking tape, again with half the tape fastened to the board, the other half fastened to the acetate.

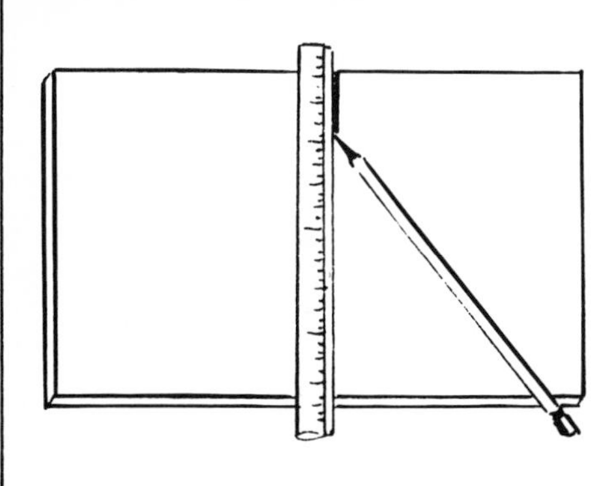

82. *Draw a line, dividing the board exactly in half.*

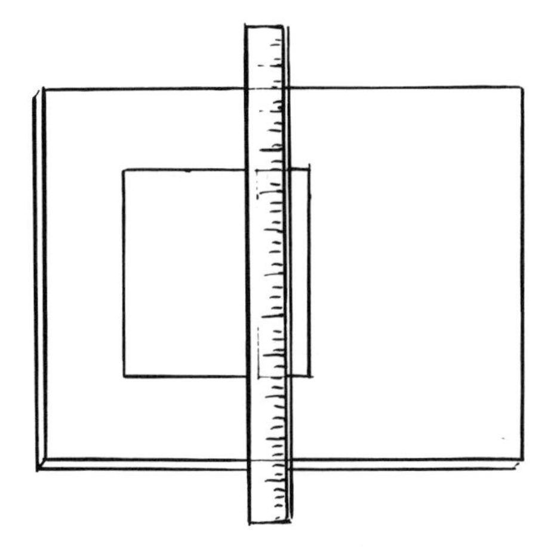

83. *Position a 4"×5" piece of acetate or celluloid on the left hand side of the board so that it is 2" from the top, side, and bottom of the edge of the board.*

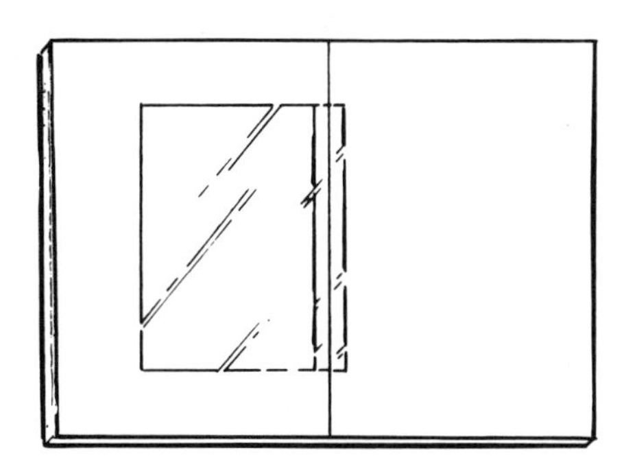

84. *Fasten the right hand edge of the acetate to the board with a 5" strip of masking tape. Flop the acetate and reinforce the hinge from behind with another strip of masking tape.*

Printing Procedure

Make a simple outline sketch on the 4" x 5" vertical card. A clean pen and ink line will be best. Flopping the acetate to the right side of the board, paste your master sketch down on the left side, the long 5" edge at the center line, again, 2" at top, side, and bottom (Figure 85).

Now flop the acetate or celluloid over the master sketch (Figures 86-87). Sprinkle a little talcum powder on the acetate (or celluloid) and rub the surface with a clean cloth. (This will give a "tooth" to the slick surface of the acetate so that you can paint on it more easily. You can also buy treated acetate which is already prepared, but is more expensive.) Dip your brush into the waterproof ink, and quickly go over the lines of the sketch you see through the clear acetate (Figure 88). Quickly place a clean 4" x 5" blank card on the right side of the board, and flop the acetate over and down on it (Figure 89). Press lightly with your cloth. Lift the acetate. If the drawing is not complete, add the additional line or lines needed, and blot again. When you've used just the right amount of ink and just enough pressure, the blotted line will be difficult to identify.

Your print should now have the look of an original sketch.

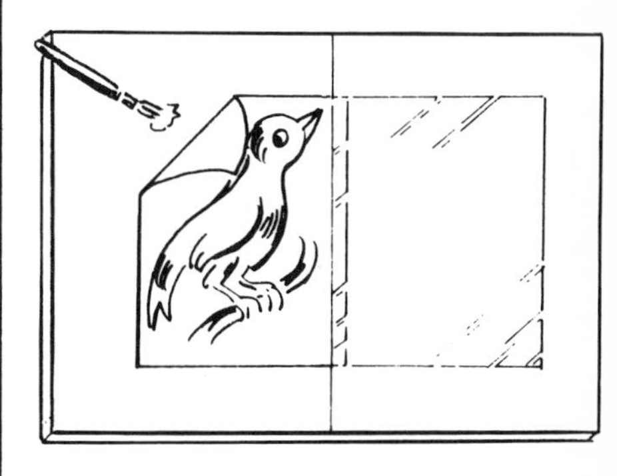

85. *Paste down your 4"×5" sketch on the left hand side of the board so that it is in the same position as the celluloid.*

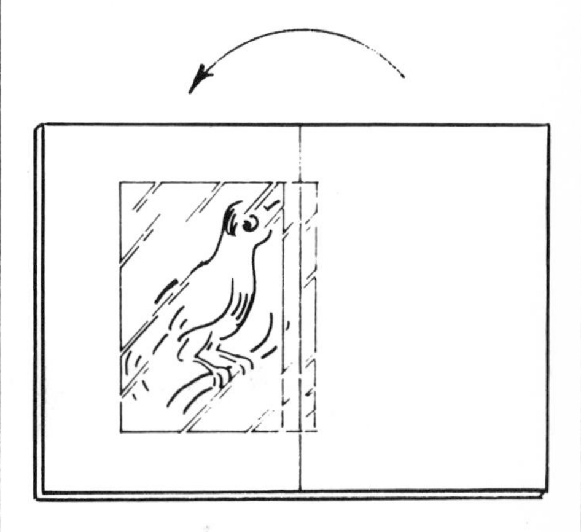

86. *Flop the acetate over the sketch and sprinkle some talcum powder on the surface of the acetate.*

87. *Rub the powdered surface with a clean cloth to give some "tooth" to the acetate.*

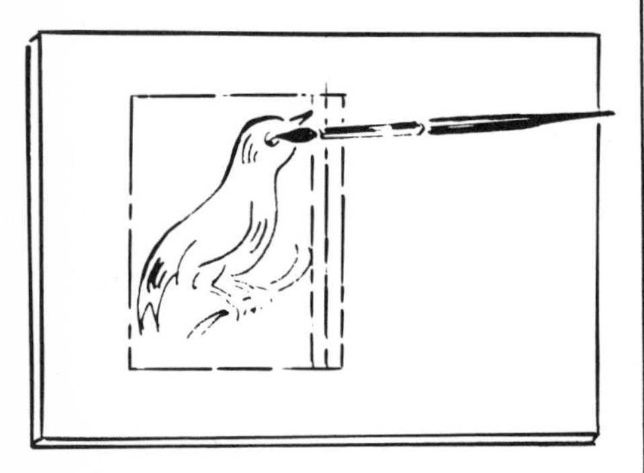

88. *Using India ink, go over the lines of the sketch you see through the clear acetate overlay.*

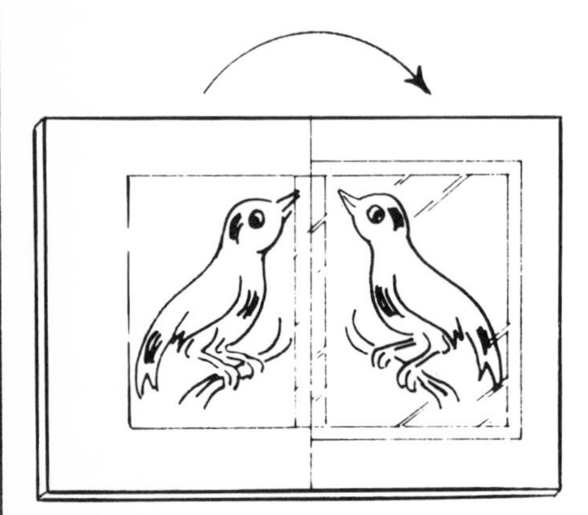

89. *Quickly place a clean 4"×5" blank card on the right side of the board and flop the acetate over and down on top of the card. Press lightly with a cloth.*

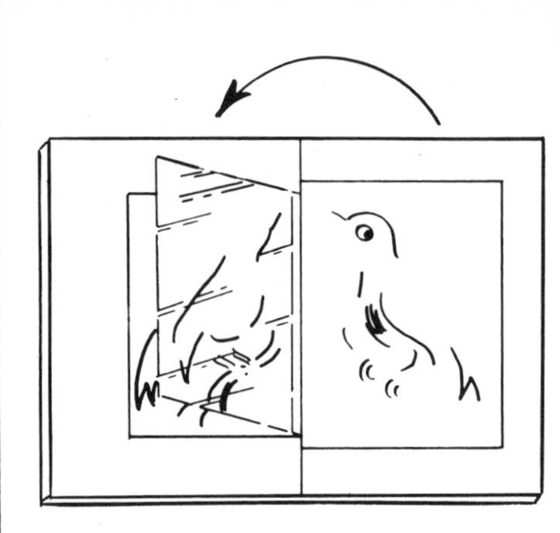

90. *Lift the acetate for checking. If the drawing is incomplete, blot again.*

91. *With the right amount of ink and pressure, the blot print should look like the original sketch.*

This blot print in black and orange has been mounted on gold foil paper and then mounted again on Japanese rice paper. By John Carlis.

A blot print made in black and orange ink on typewriter paper. The card was mounted on gift wrapping paper and then mounted again on Strathmore Double Deckle card stock. By John Carlis.

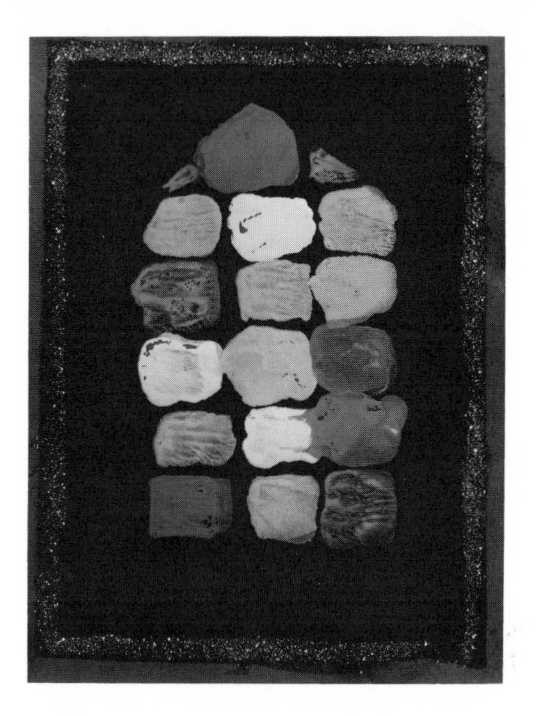

This is a colorful blot print—squares of different colors to give the effect of stained glass—with a border of silver flitter pasted around the edges. Mounted on card stock. By John Carlis.

This arresting card is actually a wash done with black ink. The blurry effect is produced by the ink saturated in the water. By Margery Soroka.

"Doggone! Forgot your birthday again!" This blot print was made in two colors, mounted on gold foil paper, with a rhinestone pasted in as an eye. By John Carlis.

This blot print was made on a photogram (see Chapter 12), with white and orange poster colors. The print was mounted on shirt cardboard which had been made into an easel back. By John Carlis.

6

Stamped Prints

We've already dealt with the most elementary form of stamp printing, the blot print. More advanced stamped prints are only a few steps removed from blotting. Lipstick pressed to a handkerchief and a sheet of paper stamped by an office rubber stamp are typical stamped prints. In this chapter, you can learn how to make greeting cards using stamped prints from easily obtained household objects. In the next chapter, we'll describe stamped prints made with linoleum and woodcuts.

92. *Here is an elementary form of stamped prints.*

Materials for Stamped Prints

Keep on hand the materials you've already used in previous chapters: the tracing paper and pencils and pens; Elmer's Glue-All, rulers and erasers, linoleum cutting tools, sheets of white and colored paper. To these add an ink slab (a sheet of glass or a slab of marble), and either oil base or water soluble inks. A brayer (or roller) is needed for all kinds of stamp printing, but you can also ink your plate with a dabber (a bunch of clean rags tied up tightly in several layers of clean cotton the size of handkerchiefs). Make sure there aren't any creases on the bottom of your dabber, because they might show up in your prints. Use strips of leather for tying up the rags, or any length of heavy twine, tied tightly.

For cleaning up oil base inks, you'll need clean rags soaked in benzene or turpentine. For cleaning up water soluble inks, use clean rags soaked with water. Benzene- or turpentine-soaked clean-up rags must be kept in a metal container that has a tightly fitting lid. This precaution prevents spontaneous combustion.

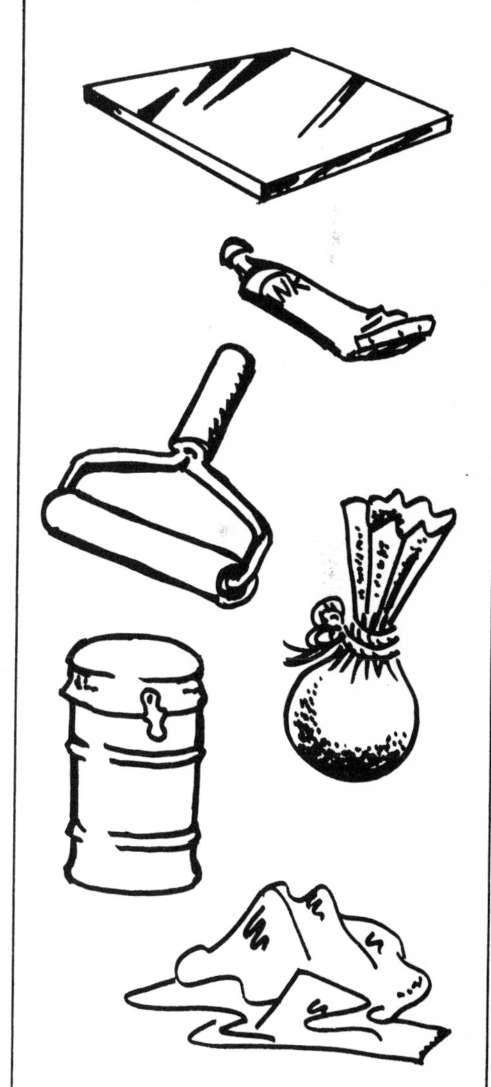

93. *Materials for stamp printing: ink slab, ink, dabber, brayer, metal container, rags.*

Printing with Ready-Made Objects

For immediate stamp printing, there is almost no end to the wide variety of ready-made units you can find around the house, at ten cent stores, or at the notion counters of department stores: checkers, jig-saw puzzle pieces, painter's graining tools, the handles or backs of brushes, the prongs of a fork, the inked rim of a water glass or a tin can for making a perfect circle, bits of screening or rubber tire or stamped metal, the bottom of a small, square bottle, the lid of a relief patterned jam jar, etc.

First, select the one or more ready-mades you plan to use. See that they're clean and dry; place them in front of you and consider what kind of pattern you're going to make, or the object you're going to "draw" with them. Squeeze out some ink from the tube onto the glass or marble slab, and coat the brayer with ink by rolling back and forth. (This procedure is called rolling up the ink.)

Holding the ready-made object in your left hand, the brayer in your right, carefully roll some ink on the surface of the object. Now press the inked surface of the ready-made object down on the paper. Then ink and print your second object (perhaps in another color), and then a third, adding to and completing your design according to your original intention. (See Figures 94-97.)

94. *Squeeze out some ink onto the glass slab.*

95. *Roll up some ink on the brayer before you print.*

96. *Roll ink onto the ready-made object. Spread the ink evenly.*

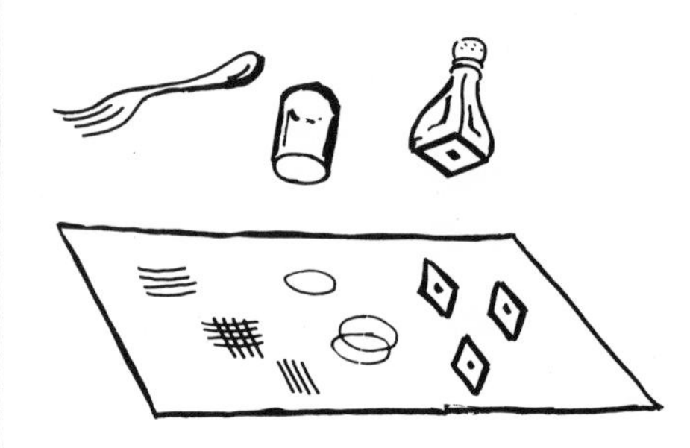

97. *After ink has been applied, press the ready-mades down on paper.*

Printing with Fruits and Vegetables

An invitation to a cook-out might feature a brand *new* kind of potato au gratin: a print made from an inked slice of Swiss cheese and an inked raw potato, shown in Figures 98 and 99.

Materials for Printing with Food

Raw potatoes cut in half
Paring knife
Pocket knife
Watercolor brushes
Jars of poster paint

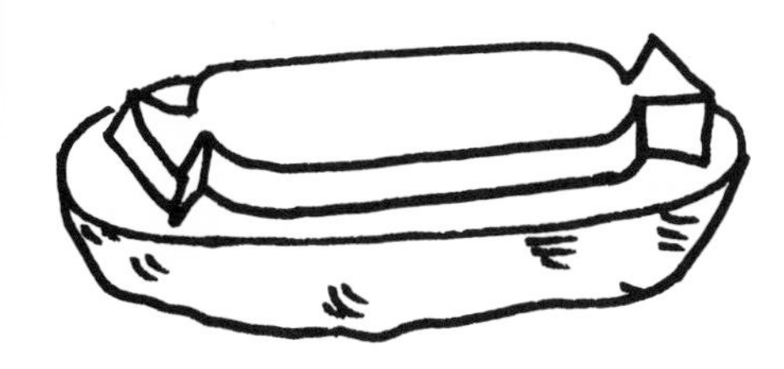

98. *Cut a potato in half and carve the shape of a frankfurter into it.*

99. *A design was cut into a piece of Swiss cheese. The cheese was inked and stamped. Potato prints form a border.*

Construction paper in various colors (available at the ten cent store)
Magic Markers and felt tipped pens
Cut ends of heads of iceberg lettuce
Halved tomato
Halved apple
Pocket mirror
Pocket mirror

Preparing the Printing Surface

Cut a potato in half with a big knife (Figure 100). Be sure to keep the cut straight so that you'll have a perfectly flat surface from which to print. With a Magic Marker or a brush dipped in poster paint, lightly outline a simple design on the potato (Figure 101). Remember, you're drawing in the reverse of what will be actually printed. Now use your mirror to check how the design will look when printed, especially important if you're using any lettering.

With your pocket knife, cut down a ¼" or so *around* your design, slanting the knife *outward* from the line you've drawn, to give the design a solid base (Figure 102). If you undercut your pattern, the edge of the potato will break off when you print.

Now, with the longer, paring knife, cut around the edge of the potato, and just to the bottom of your first outward cut.

Now, using a watercolor brush, carefully apply poster paint to the design in the potato (Figure 103). If you like, you can apply a different color to other parts of the design.

The Printing Procedure

Place a sheet of the colored construction paper on top of a cushion of ten or twelve newspaper pages, and press the inked potato gently down on the construction paper (Figures 104-105). Lift the potato, and look at your print. If the print isn't as clean as you would like, try a few trial impressions on newsprint. Then go back to the construction paper for a really clean print. Actually, printed newsprint is sometimes fun to use for greeting cards. For example, if you're announcing your move to the country, you might make a potato print on a French fold of pages from an old issue of *The Farmer's Almanac* or on the local paper's *Country and Farm Property Listings.*

100. *With a knife, cut a potato in half.*

101. *Outline a design on the potato.*

102. *Cut into the potato, slanting the pocket knife outward to give the design a solid base.*

103. *Apply poster paint to the raised portions of the design.*

104. *Press the potato down onto construction paper which has been cushioned by sheets of newspaper.*

105. *Lift the potato. If the print is rough, try a few trial impressions until you get a clean print.*

Printing with Soap Erasers

Potatoes and other vegetables disintegrate quickly, but art gum (soap eraser), handled carefully, lasts indefinitely as a printing block. Art gum has the further advantage of allowing you to cut somewhat finer detail. Soap erasers are sold in cubes 1″ x 1″ x 1″, or in 1″ x 1″ x 2″ or 3″ x 3″ x 1″ sizes. You can get a block of eraser 3″ x 6″ by gluing the sides of two 3″ x 3″ blocks together with Elmer's Glue-All.

Materials for Soap Eraser Printing

Art gum or other big erasers
Soft lead pencil
Felt tipped pens
Single-edged razor blades or X-Acto knife
Speedball linoleum cutters
Sheets of white and colored paper
Ink slab
Brayer or roller
Tubes of water soluble inks
Watercolor brushes
Jars of poster paint
Newspaper or other scrap paper
Lighter fluid or benzine
Clips of printed design from newspaper
Spoon

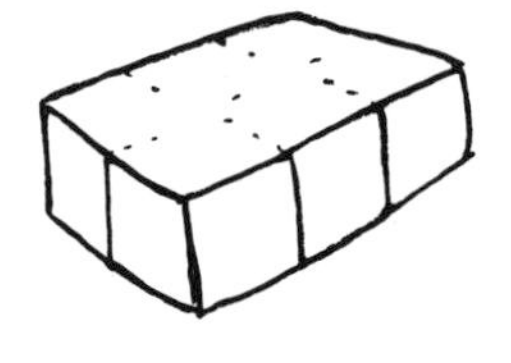

106. *Art gum comes in blocks of various sizes. You can glue several together to make a larger printing surface on the block.*

Printing Procedure

There are three ways of making a design on the eraser: you can rub down an offset tracing of your design on the eraser (see Chapter 3); you can sketch directly on the eraser, using a soft pencil or a felt tipped pen; or you can transfer, onto the eraser, an item in the morning paper. (This last method is done very easily. First select the newspaper design and cut it to size. Then squirt several generous drops of benzine or lighter fluid onto the newspaper and let it stand a moment or two Figure 108. Lay the newsprint face down on the eraser. Carefully rub the back of the newsprint with the bowl of the spoon Figure 109. The design on the newspaper will transfer to the eraser.)

Once you've made the design on the eraser, engrave the design with a shallow ($\frac{1}{16}$″) V-cut, using the small, no. 2 linoleum V-cutter (Figure 111). You can make the groove with an X-Acto knife or razor blade by making an outward, and then an inward cut, to form a V-groove.

Now gouge away — to a depth of about $\frac{1}{8}$″ — all those portions of the design which are *not* to print. You can do this easily with the no. 5 Speedball linoleum cutter (Figure 112).

Roll up some water soluble ink onto the ink slab; then, holding the eraser in your left hand, carefully roll some ink onto the surface of the design (Figure 113). Then press the inked eraser down on the greeting card paper to make a gentle impression. Lift up the eraser and you'll have the impression.

107. *Cut out an illustration from a newspaper.*

108. *Squirt several drops of benzene or lighter fluid onto the design. Let it stand momentarily.*

109. *Lay the newsprint face down on the eraser and rub the back of the newsprint with the bowl of a spoon.*

110. *Lift off the newsprint. The design will have transferred to the eraser.*

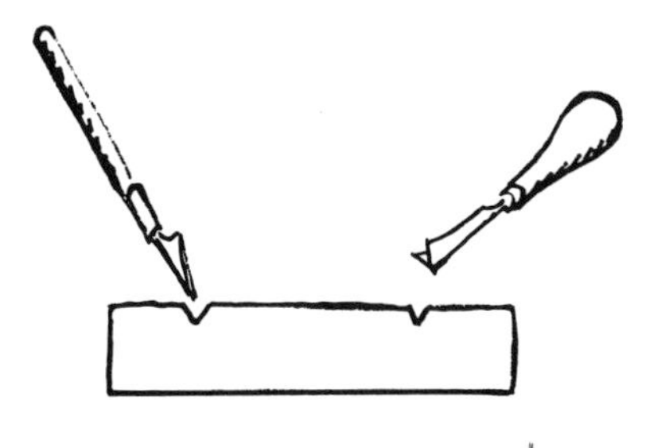

111. *Engrave the design with the no. 2 linoleum V-cutter or X-Acto knife.*

112. *Begin to remove the portions which will not print. Gouge to a depth of about ⅛". Use a No. 5 Speedball linoleum cutter.*

113. *All portions which are not printing have been removed. Roll the ink onto the raised surface of the art gum.*

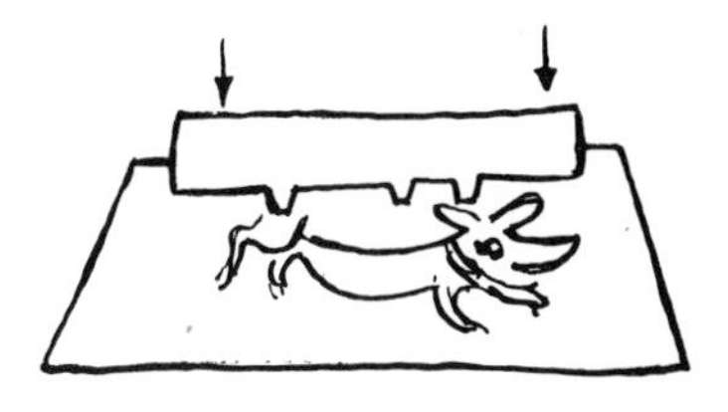

114. *Gently press the inked eraser down onto the paper.*

Printing with Corrugated Paper

So far, we've been digging into and around a design to produce a raised printing surface. Now let's try creating a printing surface by building *up* the design on a block. Attractive, modernistic abstract designs can be made for greeting cards by using several cut-out layers of thin cardboard glued down to form a design. These pieces of cardboard can be inked and printed.

Use the same materials you've used for the other stamp prints and a wood or heavy cardboard block cut to the size of your card. Also gather some pieces of thin cardboard and corrugated paper, gummed notarial seals, perhaps to add variety. A ticket punch might also come in handy.

Take the corrugated paper and cut an uneven rectangle slightly smaller than the size of your block (Figure 115). Cut a half circle just through the top layer of brown paper on the corrugated cardboard. Pull this paper back and paste down on the cardboard, making a full circle and exposing the ridges of the sandwiched layer of corrugated paper. Paste a half circle down flat (Figures 116-117). Cut other shapes from the top layer of the paper; pull up and paste down the flaps to form a pattern. Cut a little deeper and actually remove a shape or two from the corrugated paper. Punch strips of various weights of paper with a ticket punch, and paste them down. (See Figures 118-119). You'll now have a printing plate made of overlapping pieces of paper which have been built up, cut away, and punched out.

Now ink this plate with your brayer or dabber. You'll find that certain edges, folds, and cut-out portions cannot be inked because they are recessed too deep. These uninked portions will delineate your design. Lay down the plate on a piece of colored paper and print.

You can print in one of two ways: put the inked block face down on the paper, and quickly step on and off the block. Or you can place a sheet of your printing paper *over* the inked surface of your block. Take a spoon and gently rub its bowl over the paper, making sure that you rub all of the areas that are to print. Lift up a corner of the paper and look at a corner of your print. If it hasn't printed clearly enough, rub a little more. Then lift away the finished print.

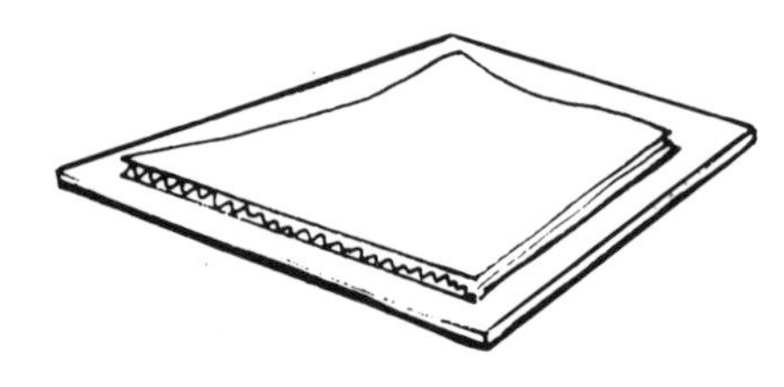

115. *Cut the corrugated paper into an uneven rectangle slightly smaller than the size of your block.*

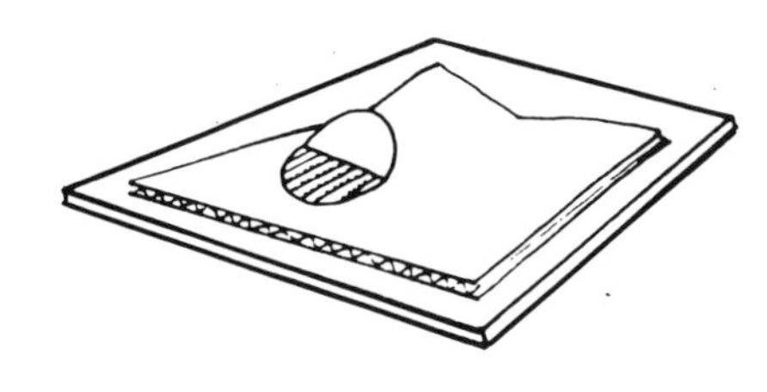

116. *Cut a half circle through the brown paper of the cardboard.*

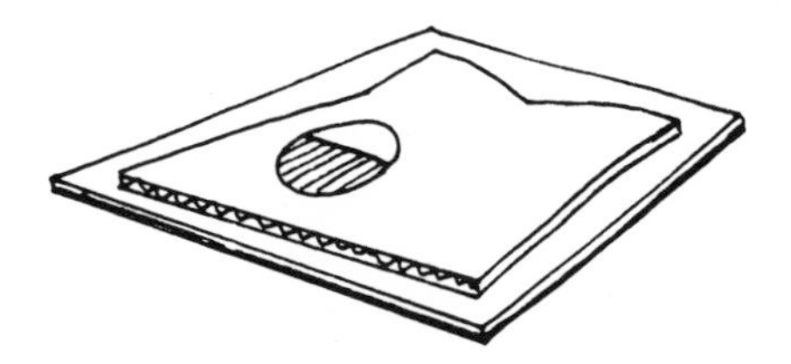

117. *Paste down the brown paper flap, making a full circle, and exposing the ridges of the corrugations.*

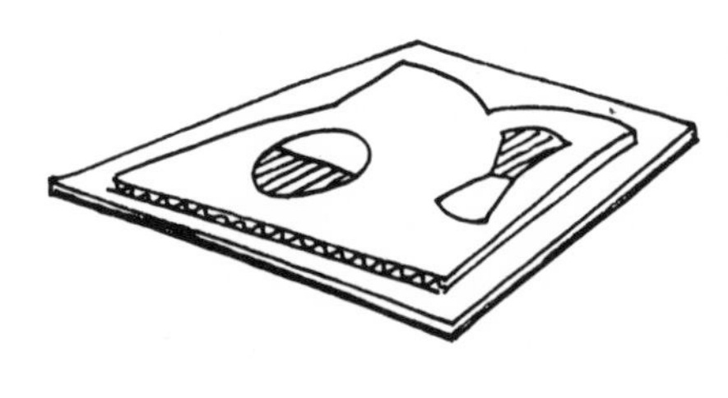

118. *The printing plate: cardboard pieces pasted down on a block. Cut other shapes into the brown paper and paste back the flaps.*

119. *Punch pieces of paper with a ticket punch and paste them down. Ink the surface and print.*

Printing with a Cardboard Mosaic

Use the same materials here as in the last project. With the X-Acto knife or a strong pair of scissors, cut a saucer-full of cardboard *tesserae*, little pieces that will make up your mosaic.

On the base block of heavy card-board or wood, make a rough sketch of your design (Figure 120). Keep the sketch broad and simple. Now, follow-ing your pattern, carefully paste down the tesserae one by one (Figure 121). You may find it necessary to cut some of the pieces at an angle to make them fit. Between each piece you paste down, leave a space of about 1/16". Perhaps you'll want to finish off your mosaic with a border of tesserae all around. This would be a nice finishing touch to the design.

Mix several saucers of various poster colors. When the paste on your mosaic is thoroughly dry, quickly paint the tesserae with a watercolor brush and poster paints (Figure 122). Turn the block face down on a piece of soft paper and step on it lightly. Your finished card should have an antique, Mediterranean look!

120. *Make a sketch of your design on a block of cardboard.*

121. *Paste down cardboard pieces to form a mosaic on the block. Leave spaces between the pieces.*

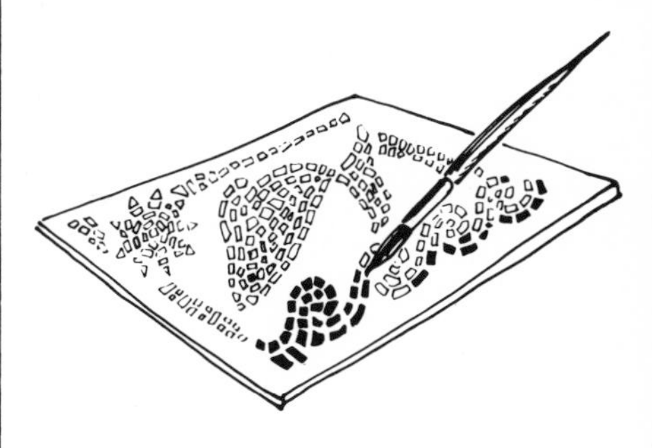

122. *Paint the tesserae with a water-color brush and poster paints.*

123. *Lay down the plate on a sheet of cardboard paper; step on it for printing.*

A colorful, rather primitive effect is achieved by printing with a cardboard mosaic. This one was printed in two colors, then mounted on a sheet of card stock. By Michael Dyne.

This card was printed on a heavy white textured watercolor paper. The artist pressed a rag soaked with oil and turpentine onto the paper. When the surface was dry, she screen-printed the tree shapes and glued on a gold star. By Margaret Rea.

These are simple potato prints. One card contains one print in one color. The other card shows two colors: red and purple. The artist used poster paints. By Sue Hodges.

7

Linocuts and Woodcuts

Having made greeting cards with tracings, rubbings, and blots, and having printed with ready-mades, cut potatoes, and art gum, you might now want to begin exploring more advanced possibilities of stamp printing: linocuts and woodcuts. Size certainly won't be a limiting factor, the way it has been with the other stamp prints you've made so far. Your design can be as small as a playing card, or as large as a window-shade!

Printing from Linoleum

Soon after its introduction into the market as a floor covering, linoleum was recognized by artists and printers as a resilient and strong printing plate which could be engraved by hand with relative speed and ease, and would stand up for long press runs. Linoleum is a mixture of ground cork and oxidized linseed oil spread over a burlap or canvas backing; it is very durable, hard, smooth, and washable, an ideal printing surface. The black and white and the multi-color linocut have been successfully explored by as diverse a range of artists as Gustav Baumann and Pablo Picasso. Although linoleum does not lend itself to the same fineness of detail as is possible with woodcuts, it is especially well suited for broader cuts and tint blocks. It's also very inexpensive.

Materials for Linocuts

Ink slab
Brayer or roller
Tubes of printing inks
Mirror
Speedball linoleum cutters
White poster color
Kitchen cleanser
Ivory Soap or a bottle of Non Crawl (available at art supply dealer)
Watercolor brush

To this list, add linoleum bought from an artist supply dealer, either in sheets or mounted on blocks. If you go directly to a floor covering dealer, ask for ¼″ thick battleship linoleum.

For under $15.00 you can buy a Speedball lightweight block printing press (available at art suppliers) which will print a block 8″ x 8″.

Preparing the Linoleum

If your lineoleum doesn't have a white surface, you should make the surface white so that you can see your sketch or offset tracing more easily. Thoroughly clean the surface, either with a benzene-soaked cloth or with a wet cloth and a bit of kitchen cleanser. Then put a little white poster paint and some water, with a drop of Non Crawl or a bit of Ivory Soap, in a saucer. Mix this solution with a big watercolor brush. With the brush, apply this thin opaque white to the surface of the linoleum (Figure 125). Let it dry.

Transfer a design to the linoleum with a tracing (Figure 126). If you want to transfer a newsprint clipping to the linoleum with lighter fluid, do not cover the surface with the white.

Now check your sketch or tracing with a mirror to get an idea of how your design will look reversed.

Using your finest V-point cutter—see Figure 127—engrave along the pencil line of your sketch, cutting to a depth of about ⅛″. Go over this small groove with a larger, round end (no. 5) cutter, cutting more deeply into the linoleum, and cutting *away* from those portions which will print. Finally, on all those portions of the block which are *not* to receive ink, cut right down to the canvas backing.

The Printing Procedure

Roll up some ink on the ink slab with the brayer (Figure 128) or dab out some ink with the dabber you've made. Roll the inked brayer over the linoleum. (If you spread the ink with a dabber, be sure to ink only the raised parts which are to print.) Place your printing paper on a cushion of newspaper sheet on the floor. Put your linocut face down on the printing paper and step on it lightly (Figure 129). If you've made a really big linocut (18″ x 24″ or so) remember that only the ball and heel of your foot give the pressure, so step carefully around on the block to give even pressure all over the entire surface.

What have you tried as your first real linocut? An exotic street scene, for a *bon voyage* greeting? A Victorian bassinette, for a birth announcement? A bouquet of flowers with lettering to announce a flower show?

Additional Colors

Don't forget, you can add hand color to your print, or you can even print from a second and third color block. If you *do* print with more than one block, be sure you register the blocks carefully so that the colors fall exactly where you want them. To do this, cut notches in each of the blocks in exactly the same places, as shown in Figure 130. Make a light pencil mark at the notch when you print the first color. Then position the notch of the second color plate with the light pencil mark so that the plates will print exactly where you want them. Do the same with the third plate.

124. *Thoroughly clean the surface of the linoleum with kitchen cleanser and a wet cloth or with benzene.*

125. *With a watercolor brush, apply a solution of white poster paint, Non Crawl or Ivory Soap, and water onto the surface of the linoleum.*

126. *Transfer your design to the linoleum with an offset tracing.*

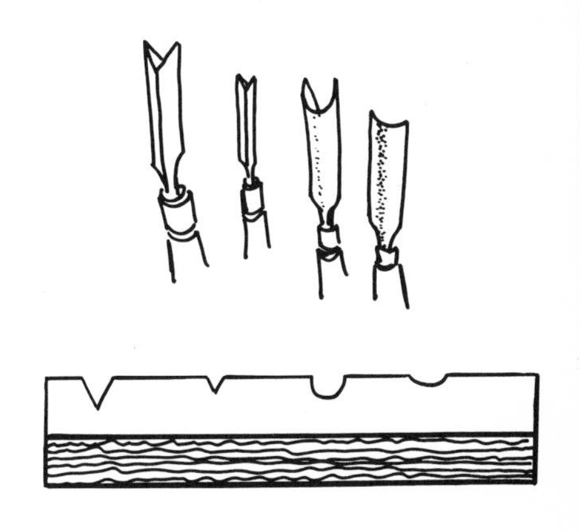

127. *These are U- and V-shaped tools and how they cut.*

128. *Roll up the ink with the brayer.*

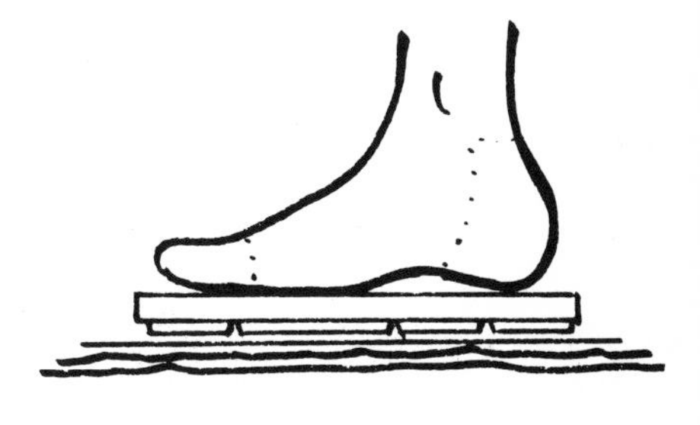

129. *Place your printing paper on a cushion of newspapers on the floor.*

130. *To insure proper registration of additional colors, notch the linoleum plates in precisely the same position so that you have a gauge for their placement.*

Making Woodcuts

Except for the fact that wood is much harder than linoleum—which means you will need cutting tools made of steel—woodcuts are very similiar to linocuts. Woodblocks for engraving are made of 1′ x 1′ sticks of maple laminated together under pressure, then sawn *across* the grain, offering a surface which, like a butcher's block, will not splinter. The wood engraver rests his block on a leather cushion as he cuts into the block. Before the invention of the photoengraved zinc block, publishers employed engravers who could quickly reproduce on the woodblocks not only ink drawings, but also crayon and pencil sketches!

Materials for Woodcuts

Laminated maple blocks sold by art suppliers or
Kiln-dried pine boards, about 1″ thick, or plywood (½″ or ¾″ thick) or scrap lumber boards
Woodcutting tools (U and V gouges of heavier metal than linocutting tools)
Sharp knife of good quality
Pencils
Tracing paper
Black India ink
Watercolor brushes
Felt tipped pens or Magic Markers
Oil or water base printer's inks
Turpentine
Old rags
Covered metal garbage can
Inking slab: piece of plate glass or marble
Brayer or inking dabber
Small mirror
Talcum powder
Newspapers, Japanese rice papers, brown kraft, or metallic papers
Sandpaper
Water
Hammer and nails
Wire mesh
Wood strips (1″ x 1″)
Old serving spoon
Wooden mallet

Preparing the Woodcut

Cut a block of wood from your board the size of your greeting (Figure 131). Transfer your sketch to the clean, dry surface of the wood or paint the design directly on the wood in black India ink or with a wide Magic Marker and a felt tipped pen (Figures 132-133). Check the design in the mirror to see how it will look in reverse (Figure 134).

Nail a strip of 1″ x 1″ wood into your work table and push the block against this strip (Figure 135). Extra care must be taken in using the sharp woodcutting tools, so always be sure to push the tool in the direction of the nailed wooden strip (Figure 136). And, as in cutting linoleum, be sure to cut *away* from the line that will print (Figure 137). Don't undercut, or the wood will break off during the printing. Using bits of wire mesh or nuts and bolts, you can hammer depressed textures into portions of your design (Figure 138). Sandpaper can roughen areas of your block as a means of contrasting smooth and rough surfaces which will pick up more or less ink from your brayer.

Inking the Plate and Printing

With the brayer, roll up either watercolor or oil based inks for printing your woodcut (Figure 139). Oil based inks are preferable if you use a dabber, since the water based inks dry faster. You might find the commercial lithographic inks the most suitable for your woodcuts, since the wood grain will need to be more carefully inked than linoleum block. Roll the brayer over your block several times before printing.

Japanese rice papers are the most sympathetic to woodcuts, but for your greeting cards try brown kraft, metallic, and suede papers as well. Use old newspapers for your first proofs; then try unprinted newsprint for your cards. Newsprint has a short life, but if you like it, use it. If you have never made woodcuts, making greeting cards on newsprint or kraft papers may one day lead you into larger "studio" prints on expensive papers.

To print, turn your inked block face down on a sheet of print paper placed on a cushion of newsprint, and step on it (Figure 141). Or place the print paper on the inked block and rub the sheet with a spoon (Figure 142). Spread your wet prints out on a table top to dry or hang them up on a line with clip clothes pins.

131. *Cut some wood from the board.*

132. *Transfer your sketch to the board with an offset tracing.*

133. *Or paint your design directly on the wood block.*

134. *Check your design in a mirror to see how it will look in reverse.*

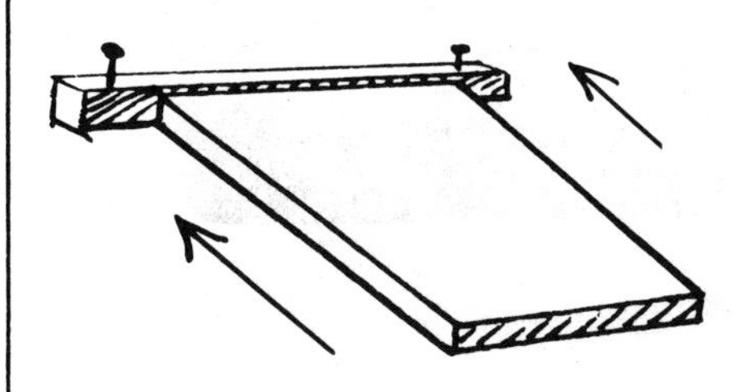

135. *Push the block against a nailed-down strip of wood.*

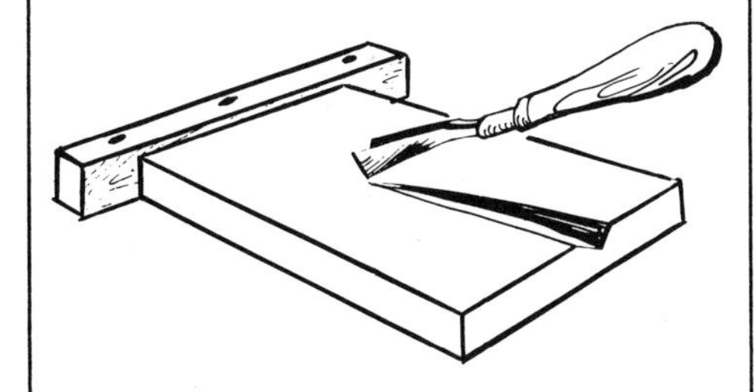

136. *Always cut the wood in the direction of the nailed strip.*

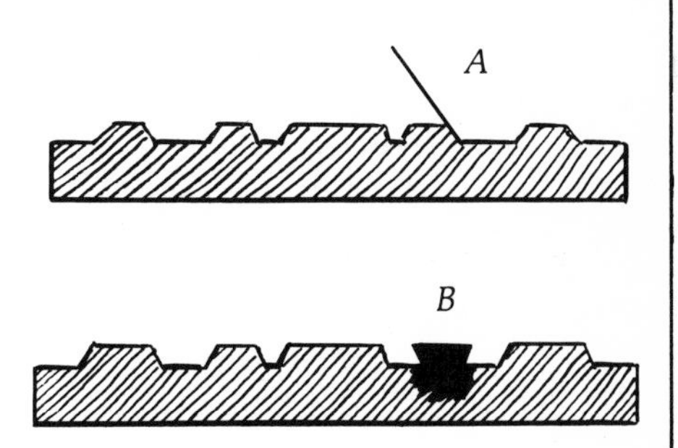

137. *Cut away from the line that will print (A). If you undercut (B), the wood will break off.*

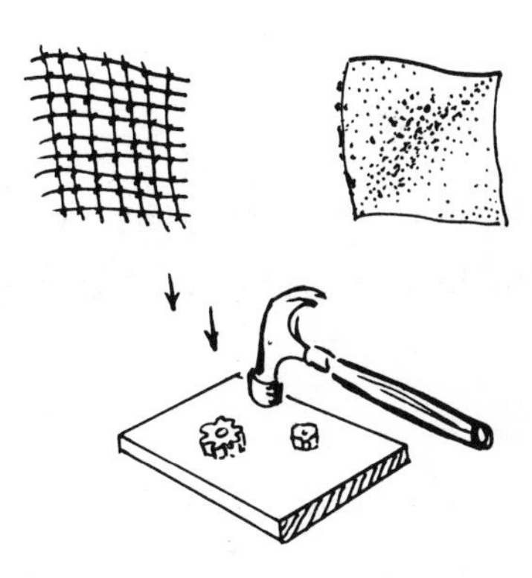

138. *You can hammer textures into areas of the block.*

139. *Remove some ink from the can with a spatula. Place it on the block and roll up the ink with a brayer.*

Making Wood Grain Prints

If you'd rather not invest in the wood-cutting tools, the attractive, highly figured, long grained markings of fir plywood can be inked and printed with a minimum of actual cutting. Soak the plywood in water, then rub it with fine sandpaper or with steel wool to raise the grain (Figure 143). Here is how you might use the wood grain in conjunction with an eraser or potato print for a card that would read: *Great Day in the Morning! I Almost Forgot Your Birthday!*

First, find a board with a knot in it, with markings going around the knot. The knot can suggest the sun, and the markings can indicate the sunrise clouds. Then saw the board to card size, keeping the long markings around the knot for suggesting the horizon, and placing the knot — the sun — a little off center (Figure 144). Now, print the block in a grayish-pink ink on a white paper.

Now take an eraser or a potato and cut a circle slightly larger than the printed knot (Figure 145). Print this circle in a bright sunrise pink directly on top of the printed knot to intensify the sun. Cut a long shape from a potato with a straight line on the bottom to suggest the horizon, and a curve on the top to suggest rising and falling hillsides. Print this in a blue-gray beneath the sun once or twice, moving it along to indicate the rolling hills. When the print is dry, letter your greeting with a pink Magic Marker at the bottom: *Great Day in the Morning!* and inside the fold — *I Almost Forgot Your Birthday!*

140. *In woodcuts, you can use printed and unprinted newsprint, or a roll of brown kraft wrapping paper. Other papers will also work well.*

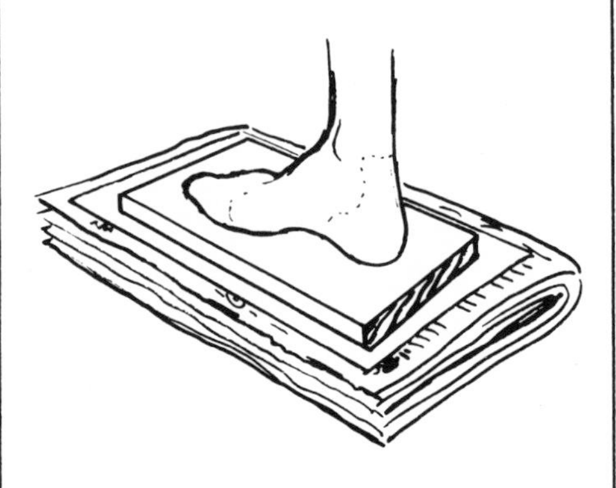

141. *To print, place the block face down on the sheet of paper which is cushioned by newspapers. Step on the block lightly.*

142. *You can also print by rubbing the sheet with the bowl of a spoon.*

143. *Wet the board with water to bring up the grain.*

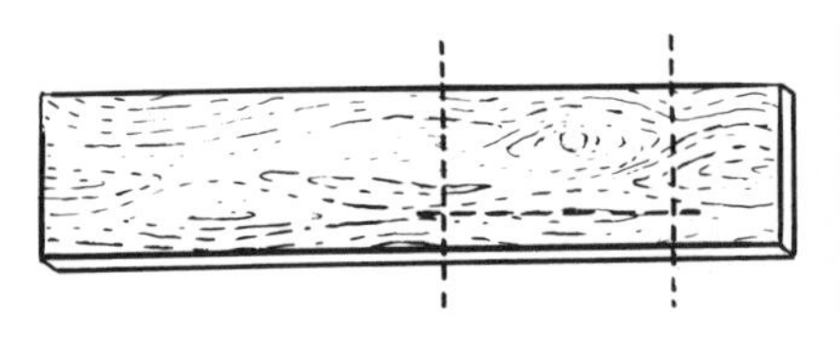

144. *Find a section of the board with a knot in it and saw the wood to card size. Place the knot slightly off-center.*

145. *From potatoes, cut a circle (for the sun) and a long, curved shape (for the low mountains and horizon) with a paring knife.*

146. *Superimpose the potato prints over the wood print to achieve an effect something like this.*

With this original Woodcut
Norman & Diana Kent
Send You Season's Greetings

The woodcut is a traditional medium for religious holiday cards, dating back to the middle ages. By Norman Kent.

Precise color registration in printing is important when you print in more than one color. Here is a proof of a black plate. Six colors were added to the black, all in good register. By George R. Fernandez.

On the left is the block which was carved for a woodcut. On the right is the final print. By John Carlis.

This woodcut is printed in two rather unusual colors: turquoise blue (birds) and olive green (trees). By Robert Quackenbush.

This is a two-color linoleum print. The words "Peace on Earth" were set on a linotype machine and attached to the linoleum block for printing. By Jim Marsh.

There is a rather interesting mottled effect in the heavy coating of ink which this artist created by printing two impressions with a linoleum block. By Jim Marsh.

This is a handsome linoleum print made in five brilliant colors and printed on a soft rice paper. By George R. Fernandez.

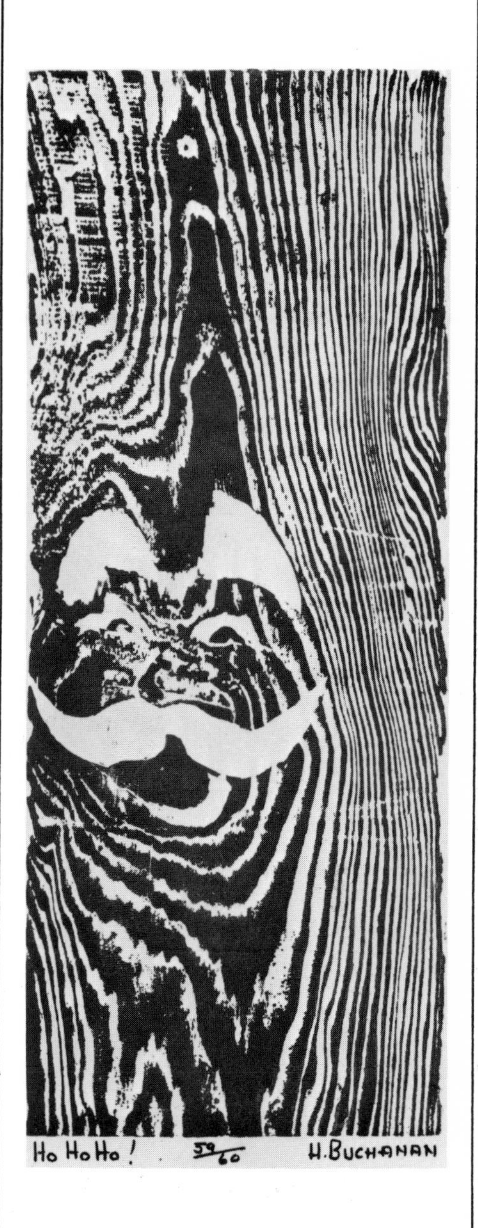

Beach wood — which had been grained by salt water and sand — provided the printing surface for this card. The plank was cut to size, the features on Santa's face were cut out with an X-Acto knife, and the print was made on rice paper with oil based printer's ink. By Helen A. Buchanan.

This woodcut has been printed in two colors on a soft rice paper, then mounted inside a French fold card. By Walter Ferro. Collection, Norman Kent.

Interesting linear effects can be achieved by wood engravings. This card was printed in orange on a warm beige paper. By John Carlis.

This handsome partridge in a pear tree was printed from a wood block, in black on a light rice paper. By Ann Schneeberg.

Your own home can provide a good motif for a Christmas card. By Ernest Watson. Collection, Norman Kent.

This wood engraving is a difficult medium for the beginner, but you can achieve similar effects on very old, very hard linoleum. By Lynd Ward. Collection, Norman Kent.

This abstraction of a biblical theme was printed in three colors from a linoleum block, on a card stock. By Jim Marsh.

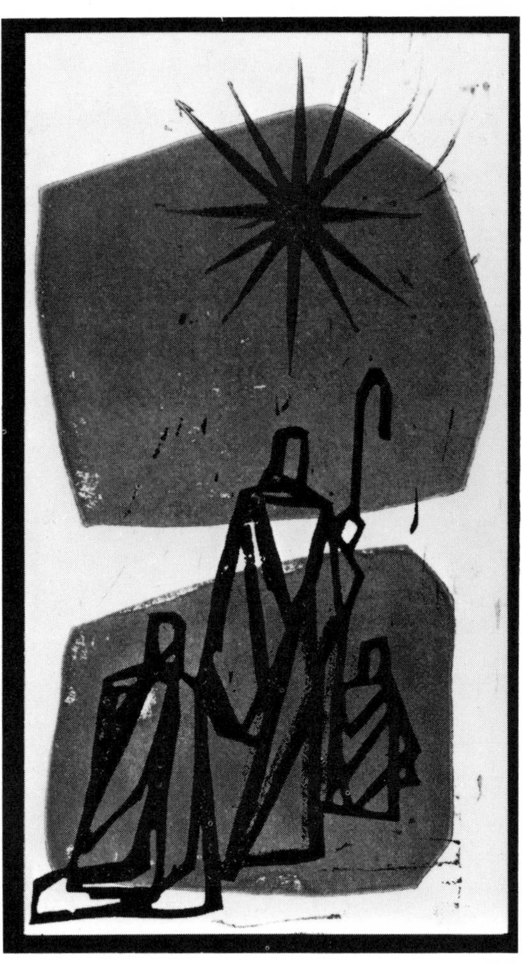

This woodcut was printed on a rough, absorbent, handmade Japanese paper which adds texture to the bold strokes of the knife. By Anthony Sarris. Collection, Norman Kent.

This linocut of the Archangel Michael fighting the antichrist, is a design based on a Russian church flag of the 16th century. By Fritz Eichenberg. Collection, Norman Kent.

This is a wood print made on driftwood. Notice the natural grain of the wood which has been used to create an image of the three wise men. By Jessamine Haines.

8

Monotypes

As the name suggests, a monotype is a print that gives only a single impression. To make a monotype, you paint on a sheet of glass, lay a sheet of paper over the wet paint, and press down with enough pressure to transfer the paint to the paper. When the paper is pulled from the glass, you'll have an interesting and special effect. For greeting cards, the single print produced by the monotype gives you yet another graphic direction for your magic bag of greeting card tricks that is going to have your friends asking, "How in the world did you do it?"

Materials for Monotypes

Sheet of glass (13″ x 16″)
Tubes of artists' oil paints
Small bottle of oil paint dryer
Oil painting brushes
Sheet of marble or glass to use as a palette
Soft lead pencil (2B or 3B)
Some sheets of white paper and a sheet of tracing paper
Tinted or colored paper slightly larger than 13″ x 16″ (midnight blue or light gray is suggested for this design)
Scissors
Brass-edged ruler
Razor blades, or an X-Acto knife
Turpentine and clean rags

Preparing the Design

Using a ruler, measure out a sheet of white paper 12″ x 15″, dividing it by pencil into fifteen equal sections; that is, three 4″ sections along the 12″ end of the paper, and five 3″ sections along the 15″ side. (See Figure 148.) Each section will then be 3″ x 4″.

Work out an idea for your design (Figure 149). Let's say you've made a

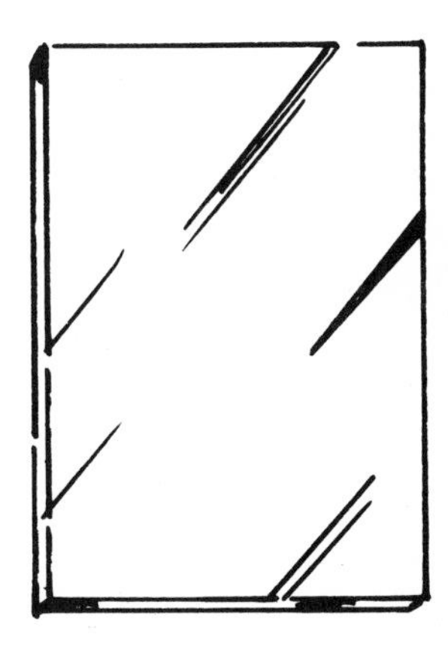

sheet of glass

marble palette

147. *Here are the materials you'll need for monotypes.*

pencil sketch of a pine tree on a snowy slope which is set against a sky that will be light blue. Draw this design on one of the sections within an area of 3″ x 4″. (It can be larger if you like; you might want to divide the 12″ x 15″ area into quarters or eighths instead of fifteenths.) Within the grid of fifteen squares, transfer your sketch by rubbing down the design fifteen times (see Chapter 3), so that the grid will contain fifteen copies of the same design. (See Figure 150.)

Now place the sheet of clear glass directly over the patterned grid of design repeats (Figure 151). Squeeze out some white oil paint on your palette, some deep green, and some blue. Mix blue and white to get a light blue, and mix a drop or two of dryer in with the dark green, the light blue, and the white.

Printing Procedure

By hand, quickly paint fifteen pictures directly onto the glass, using the transferred pencil sketches seen through the glass as a guide (Figure 152). Use a light blue for the sky, deep green for the pine tree, and white for the snowy slope. You also might want to paint in other elements — a bird, a sled, or a star. (Avoid any lettering because this will be printed in reverse.)

Place a sheet of colored paper — midnight blue, or light gray — over the wet oil paint on the glass. Press down smoothly, using a clean cloth in order to be sure all the paper is making contact with the glass (Figure 153). Starting at a corner, carefully pull the paper away (Figure 154). Set the printed paper aside to dry, clean the glass with a little turpentine and cloth (Figure 155). Paint and print again.

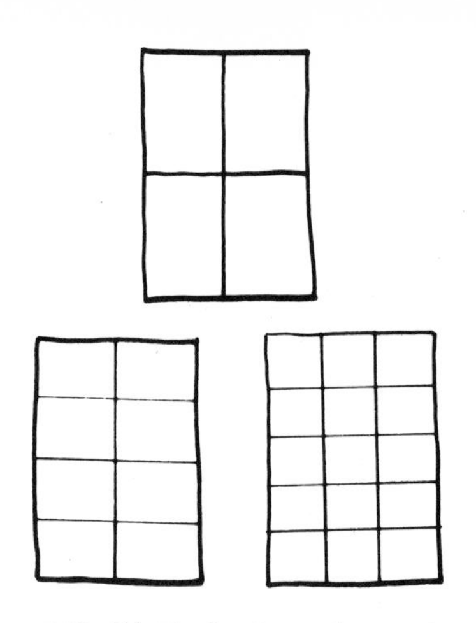

148. *Divide the sheet of paper into window pane sections.*

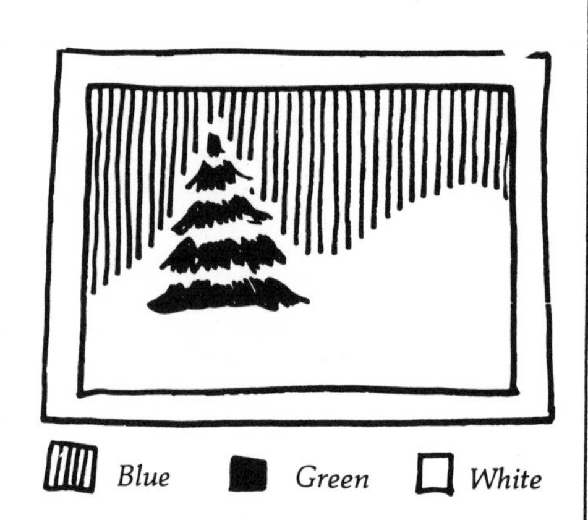

149. *Make up a sketch for the monotype.*

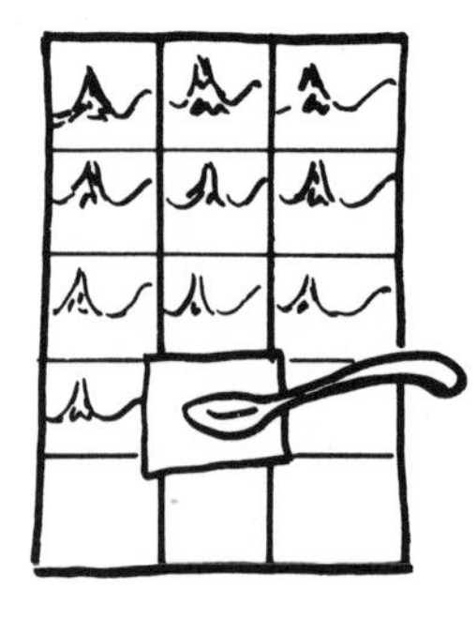

150. *Transfer the design to the grid, so that it repeats several times.*

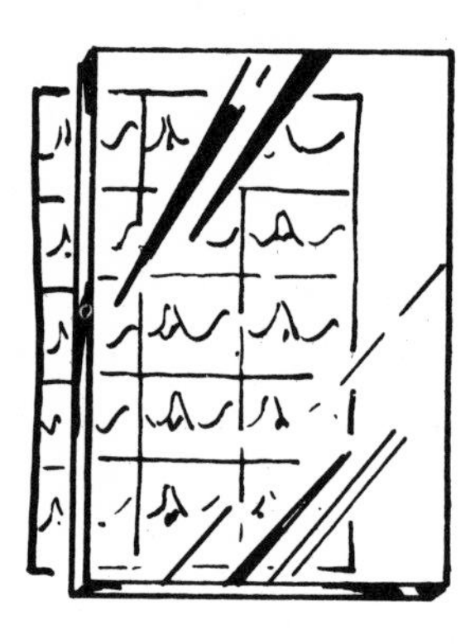

151. *Place a sheet of glass squarely over the design.*

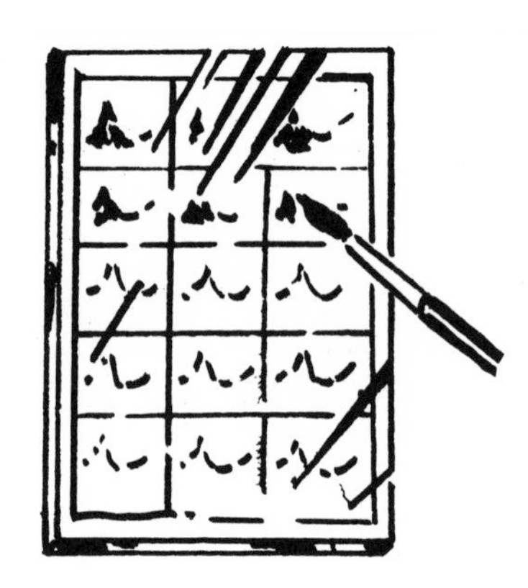

152. *Quickly paint the designs on the glass, following the sketches you see through the transparent surface.*

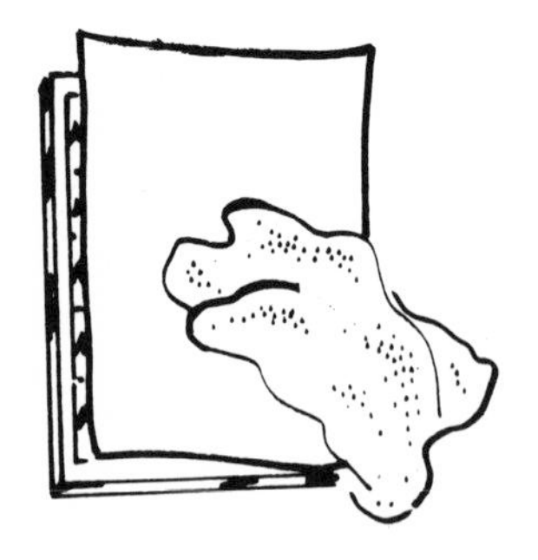

153. *Using a clean cloth, press down a sheet of paper on the glass.*

154. *Carefully pull the paper away from the glass.*

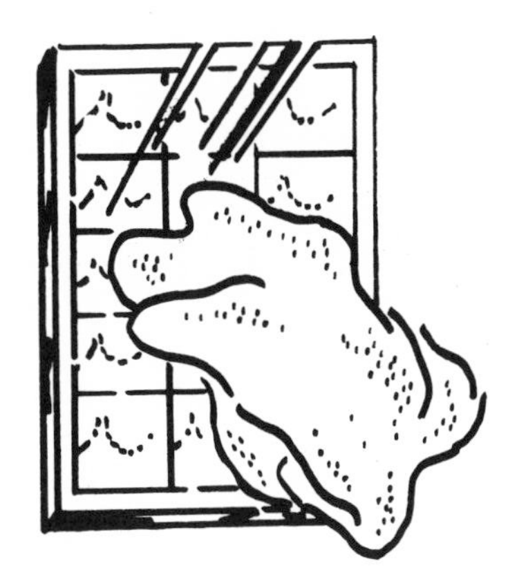

155. *Clean the glass with turpentine-soaked rag.*

Trimming the Card

After the printed sheets have dried, cut apart the multiple prints with scissors, or an X-Acto knife, or a single-edged razor blade, using a brass-edged ruler as a guide (Figure 156). Three of these sheets, cut apart, will give you forty-five little monotypes. (Naturally, if you want to make larger cards you can! You might want to divide a 12" x 15" surface into quarters or eighths, rather than fifteenths as shown here.)

Paste the prints on folds of colored or metallic paper or on a stand-up box fold as shown in Figure 157.

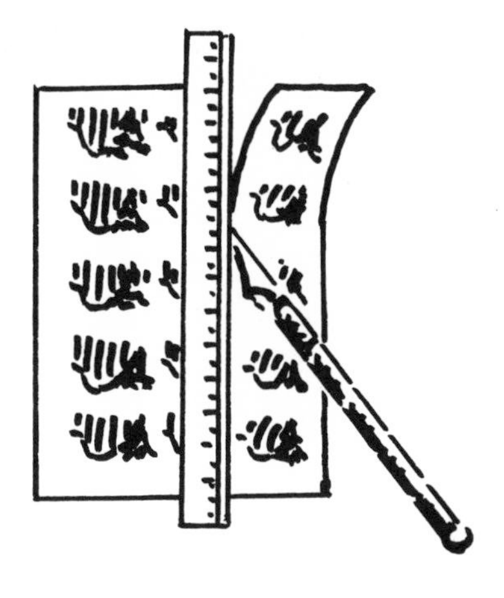

156. *Trim apart the multiple prints.*

157. *Paste the print on a box fold card.*

"We're spouting with joy!" This monotype was printed on construction paper, then mounted on a card stock. A signal dot was pasted onto the eye. By John Carlis.

A blurry effect has been created by this monotype printed on a smooth parchment paper. By John Carlis.

A monotype for Mother's Day, printed on brown kraft paper. A free-hand border of double lines was drawn with a felt tip pen. By John Carlis.

For Father's Day, this monotype was printed on brown kraft paper which was mounted on gift wrapping paper, then mounted again on a green card stock. By John Carlis.

The splotches and blurs lend a festive quality to this invitation to a costume party. By John Carlis.

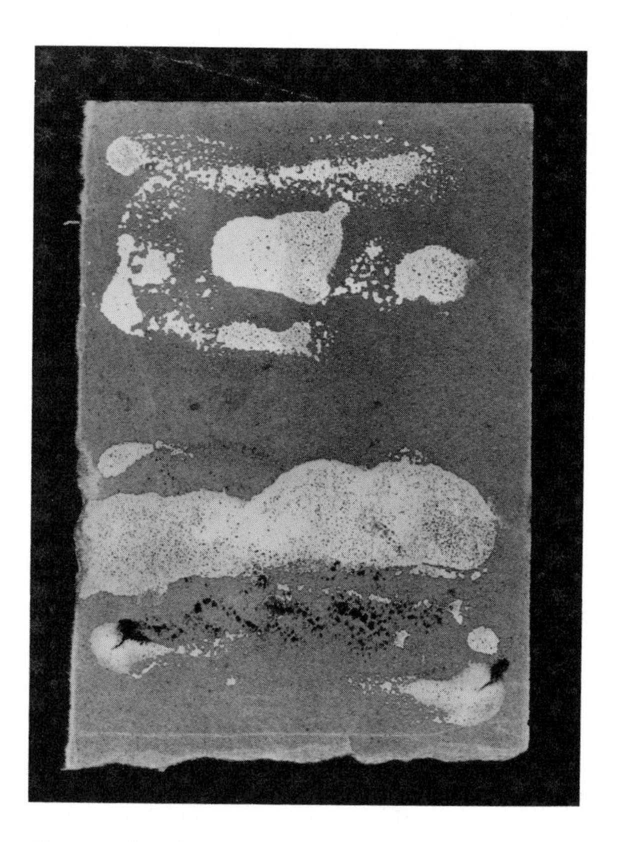

The artist here has created a curious effect by printing a monotype on sandpaper, then mounting the print on a contrasting gift wrapping paper. By John Carlis.

The linear elements in this card were silk screened. For the swirly background, the artist applied oil paint to Plexiglas with his thumb. He then pressed the card to the surface of the Plexiglas to pick up the paint. By Jim Marsh.

9

Etching

The prints you've made so far — potato printing, linocut engraving, eraser printing, etc. — have been produced by inking a raised surface. With monotypes, you laid the paper over a flat slick surface which was coated with paint. Etching is different from all these printing techniques. First, the image is incised with scratched grooves, the ink is caught in the recessed scratched grooves, and all portions above the groove are wiped clean. A studio etching plate is a smooth sheet of copper, coated with wax. The artist draws through the wax coating with a sharp point. He then places the plate into an acid bath. The acid eats away the copper wherever the sharp point has removed wax, and will form a groove in the copper which can later receive ink. We will simplify this procedure by eliminating acid and the copper, and instead we will cut directly into a sheet of plastic with a sharp point. This is a fast and fun method for making greeting cards, and soon you, too, can start asking people up to see your etchings.

Materials for Etching

- Some pieces of heavy celluloid or clear plastic the thickness of cardboard available from any major art supplier (see shopping guide.)
- Darning needle or any similar object with a sharp point
- Wooden dowel (6″ long, ½″ in diameter)
- Old-fashioned clothes wringer or a screw press: anything providing pressure
- Brass-edged ruler
- Single-edged razor blade or X-Acto knife
- Sheet of fine sandpaper
- Linoprinting ink in a deep brown color
- Watercolor paper
- Blotters
- Turpentine and clean cloths for cleaning up
- Dabber
- Ivory-toned paper

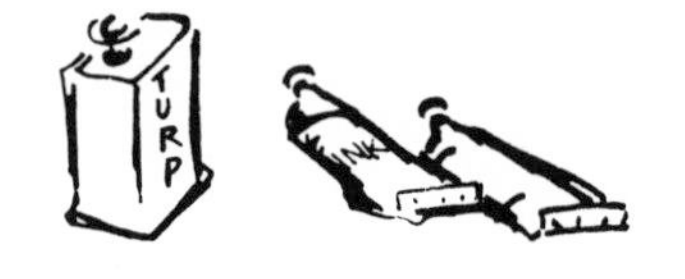

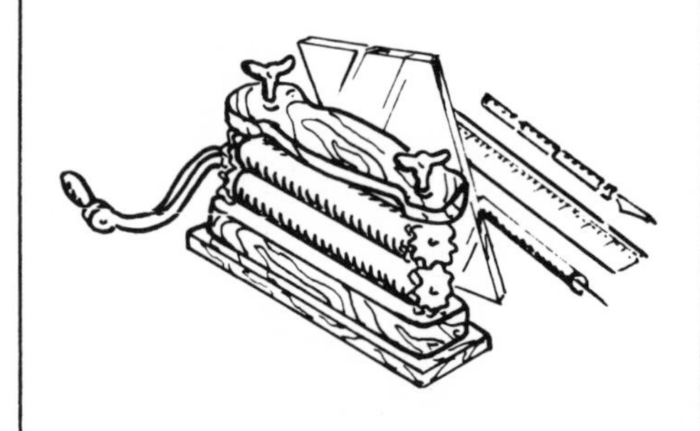

158. *Materials for etching: clothes wringer, clear plastic, etching tool, ruler, X-Acto knife, turpentine, ink, rags, watercolor paper, blotters.*

Preparing the Plate

First consider your design. How about a sketch? Perhaps you can draw your living room, your dog or cat sleeping by the fireplace. In Warren, Pennsylvania, where I visit from time to time, artists often drive up to the heights and paint or sketch the panorama of the town and the meandering Allegheny River below. On the other hand, you don't have to sketch from real life scenes. You might prefer to create an abstraction in a pattern of lines. As I suggested earlier, nothing prevents you from adapting any photograph or print you happen to like.

After you've made your design, you can make the plate. Cut your plastic to size, say 4″ x 6″, using a brass-edged ruler as a guide and an X-Acto knife or a single-edged razor blade. It won't be necessary to cut all the way through the plastic (see Figure 161); simply score the surface (cut into the plastic with the blade along the ruler). Now hold the plastic firmly on each side of the scoring and snap for a clean break (Figure 162). Sandpaper the corners of the plate.

Now make your etching tool: take a darning needle or any object with a sharp metallic point — the pointed end of a compass or one end of a divider will also do — and stick it into a wooden dowel 6″ long, ½″ in diameter, the sharp point out. The dowel will be the handle of your etching tool. In any art materials store you can also buy a ready-made point attached to a holder.

Now fasten your sketch to the underside of the plastic with four little dots of paste (Figure 164). Hold the etching point as you would a pen or pencil. Scratch the design on the surface of the plastic, following the lines of your sketch below (Figure 165).

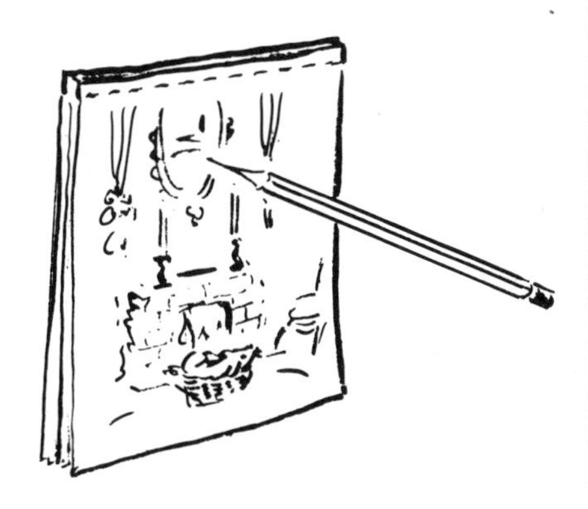

159. *Perhaps you'll want to sketch your livingroom.*

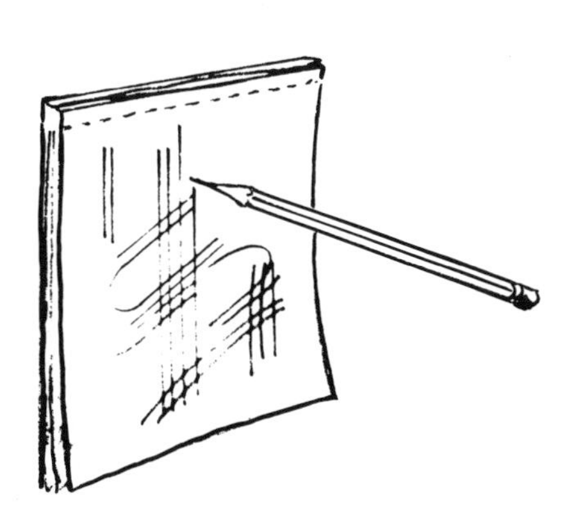

160. *Or perhaps you'd like to create an abstraction.*

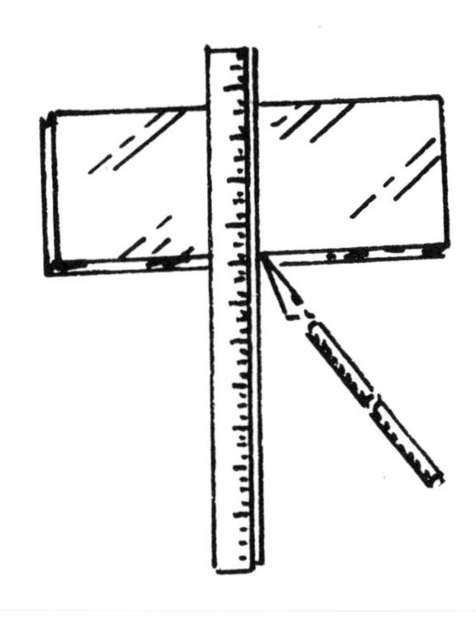

161. *Score the plastic with the knife.*

162. *Snap the plastic apart to make a clean break.*

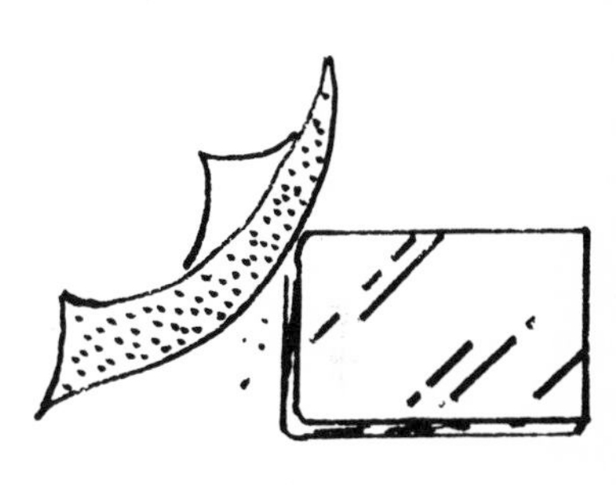

163. *Using sandpaper, round off the corners of the plate.*

164. *Fasten your sketch to the underside of the plastic.*

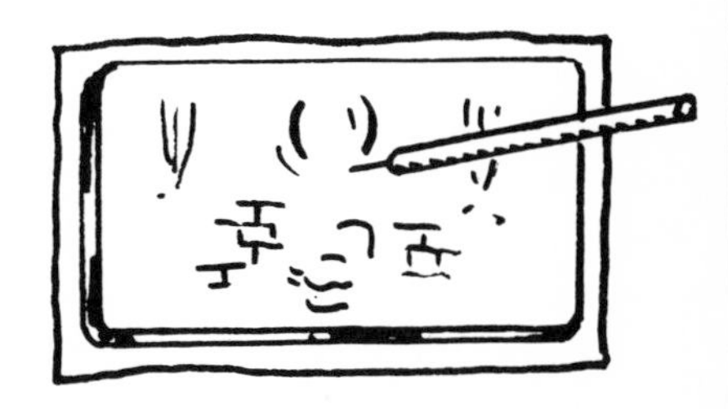

165. *Scratch the design on the surface of the plastic, following the lines of your sketch below.*

Inking the Plate

When you'd inked your linoleum cut, you inked a *cameo*, or a raised line. Now for your etching, you will ink an intaglio line, a line cut *into* the surface of the plate. Daub some of the brown printer's ink into the grooves on your plastic plate (Figure 166). Remove excess ink from the surface with a clean cloth; the scratched lines filled with ink will indicate — in reverse, of course — how your finished print will look (Figure 167). You may want to scratch in a few more lines here and there, filling these with ink also. You can leave atmospheric tone on the plate also, by leaving some ink on the raised surface of the plate: across the sky perhaps, or maybe as shadows in the foreground.

The Printing Procedure

Dampen the paper you are using for your cards. (Pass a wide, wet watercolor brush over the sheet — as shown in Figure 168 — and leave the dampened paper between two sheets of blotting paper. Dampen a good supply of paper, storing it in a pile of alternating sheets of blotting and printing paper.)

Take one sheet of the damp paper and carefully place it over the inked plate. Make a paper and plate sandwich, placing the paper and plate between several sheets of clean, dry blotting paper (Figure 169). Carefully run the sandwich through the clothes wringer, or press in the screw press (Figure 170). Remove the print, ink up the plate again, and continue to complete your edition.

166. *Daub the printer's ink into the grooves of the plastic plate.*

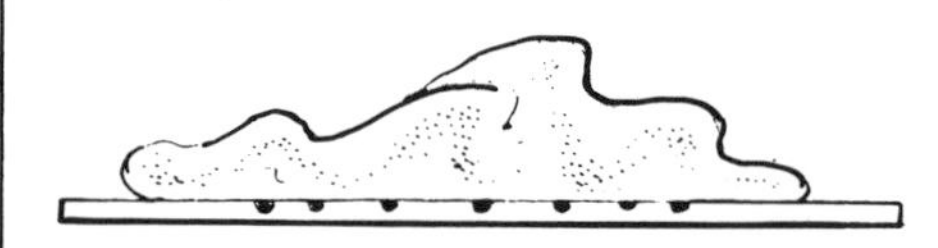

167. *Remove ink from the surface of the plate with a clean cloth.*

168. *Dampen the paper by passing a wet watercolor brush up and down the sheet. Store the damp paper in a pile of alternating sheets of blotting and printing paper.*

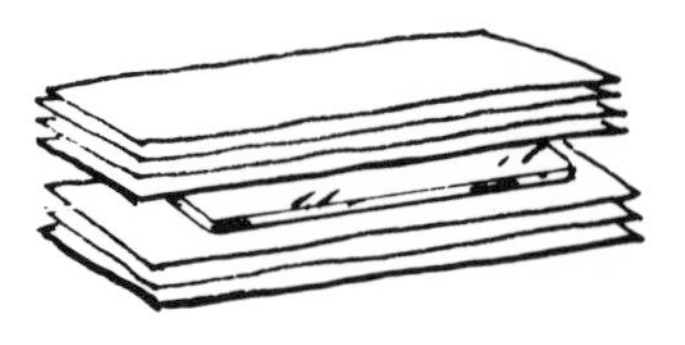

169. *Put a sheet of damp paper over the plate and insert the two between several sheets of blotting paper.*

170. *Carefully run the sandwich of plate, paper, and blotters through the wringer or press.*

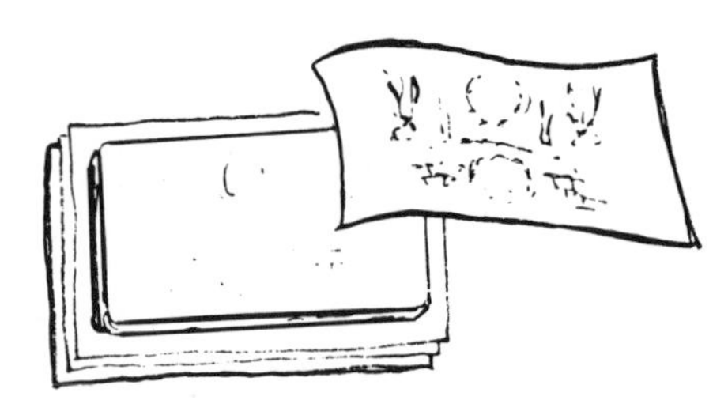

171. *Remove the print from the plate.*

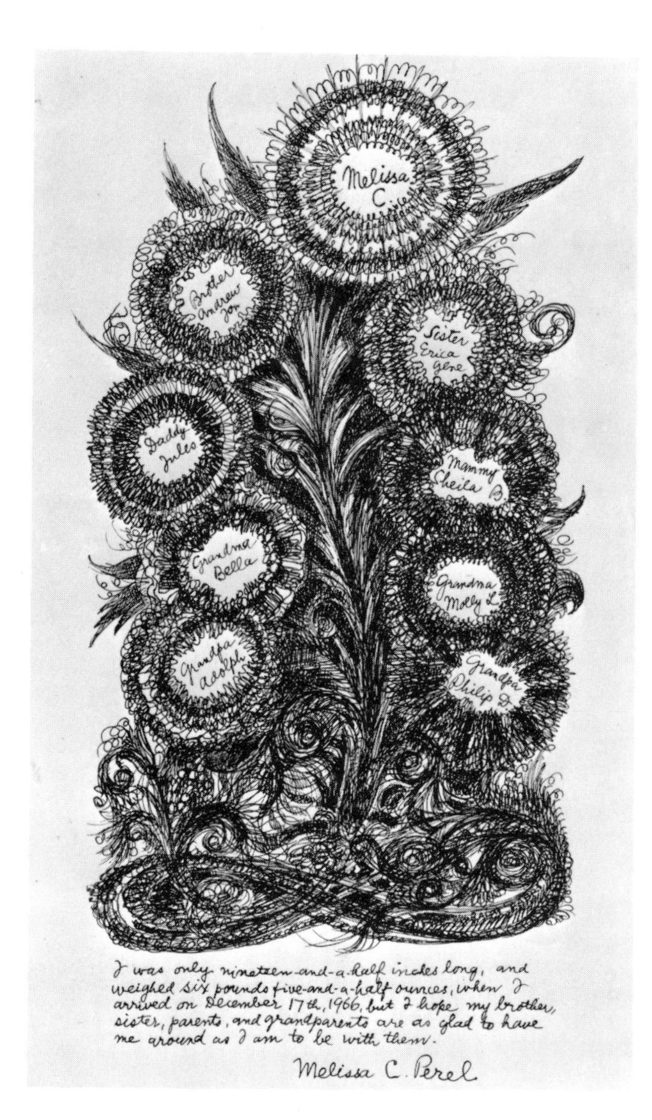

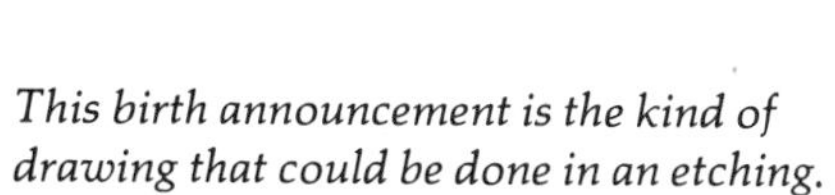

This birth announcement is the kind of drawing that could be done in an etching. By Ralph Fabri. Collection, Jules Perel.

Like this pen drawing, etchings are characterized by a strong linear quality. Hand coloring will add vitality to the sketch. By Warren Chappell. Collection, Norman Kent.

10

Stencils

Stencils are a form of printing in which the unprinted portions are masked out and the ink or paint passes through the available openings onto the printing surface.

The sign *Wet Paint* is probably the most familiar stencil we know (see Figure 172); the painter passes his brush over a card in which the letters have been cut out. The paint goes through the cut-out shapes of letters onto the sign beneath. Unlike stamp printing, only the cut-out part prints, so it is of primary importance to remember that the loop of the *P* in *Paint*, for example, has to be supported by little bridges or "ties." Without the ties, the entire loop of the *P* would drop out of the stencil and you would no longer have an outlined letter. (See Figure 173.) So a stencil may be cut out of a thin sheet of oiled paper, or a sheet of thin metal or plastic through which paint is either daubed with a brush or sprayed. In fact, a stencil can be *any* object which masks out some portions and permits passage of ink or paint through others. For example, if you placed a plastic fern on a sheet of white paper and sprayed the fern and the paper with paint, then lifted up the fern from the paper, you would have a white image of the fern pattern on the paper. In other words, you can make a stencil print by daubing paint with a brush or spraying paint from a toothbrush or pressurized can against *anything* which masks the paper, leaving an image when the mask is removed.

Stencil printing is a method entirely unlike anything we have done so far; what you've learned in previous chapters in the way of creating a pattern and mixing and using colors now ought to be of real service to you in the preparation of a stencil.

In the next chapter I will describe silk screens, a stencil supported on a taut, open mesh though which paint is forced with a squeegee. In this chapter, I will describe other forms of stencil printing.

172. *The Wet Paint sign is probably the most familiar stencil.*

173. *Ties secure the loop of the P to the stem of the P. Without the ties, the loop would drop away from the stencil.*

Materials for a Sprayed Stencil Print

Plastic snowflake 3″ or 4″ in diameter (see shopping guide)
X-Acto knife or sharp scissors
Can of pressurized spray "snow"
Deep blue paper
Toothbrush
White ink or white poster color
Small watercolor brush
Scrap cardboard
Stencil paper

Making the Sprayed Stencil Print

First cut the blue paper to 4″ x 8″ or 5″ x 10″, and fold the sheet in two. If you don't have a plastic snowflake on hand, you can make your own. Take a sheet of heavy paper and cut a design, such as the six-pointed star illustrated in Figure 174, in a repeat pattern, much the way you would cut out a paper doll. You will have a sheet, the cut-out portion of which is a design of a six-pointed star. (Always be sure to cut your stencils against scrap cardboard to avoid marring your desk or work table.) Now place the stencil on the fold of blue paper (Figure 176).

Spray the paper lightly with canned snow (Figure 177), let it dry a bit, and carefully take away the stencil. Or, you can print with a toothbrush rather than a pressurized can (Figure 178). Mix up some white ink or white poster color with enough water to give it a cream-like consistency. With your watercolor brush, apply the white mixture to your toothbrush. Hold the toothbrush, bristles up, in your left hand. Snap the tip of your right index finger across the wet bristles of the toothbrush, causing the paint to spatter. (Incidentally, this is a good way to print most stencils. Keep on hand many toothbrushes, for as many colors as you think your design needs.) When you lift away the stencil, you will see the white design of your snowflake printed on the blue paper.

Using your watercolor brush, write your greeting inside the fold in white ink or in poster paint.

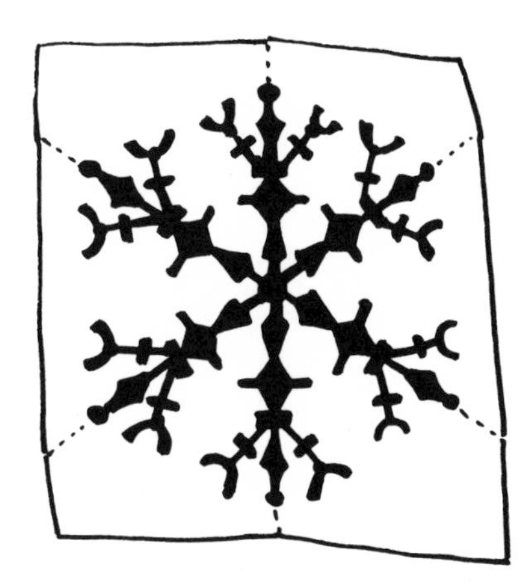

174. *Fold a sheet in six's. Sketch and cut out a six-pointed star.*

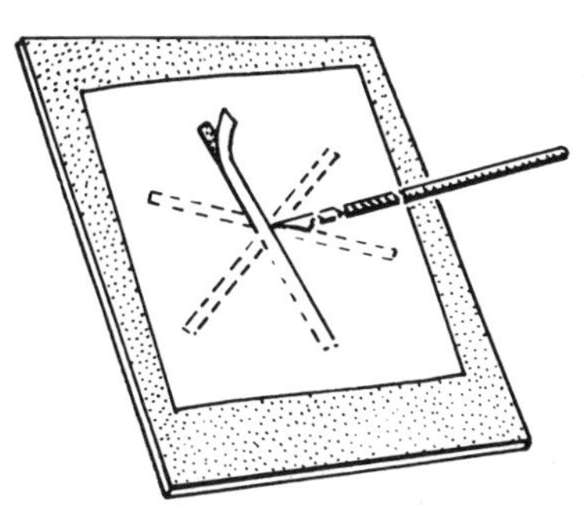

175. *Cut your stencils against scrap cardboard to avoid marring your desk or table.*

176. *Place the stencil on a fold of blue paper.*

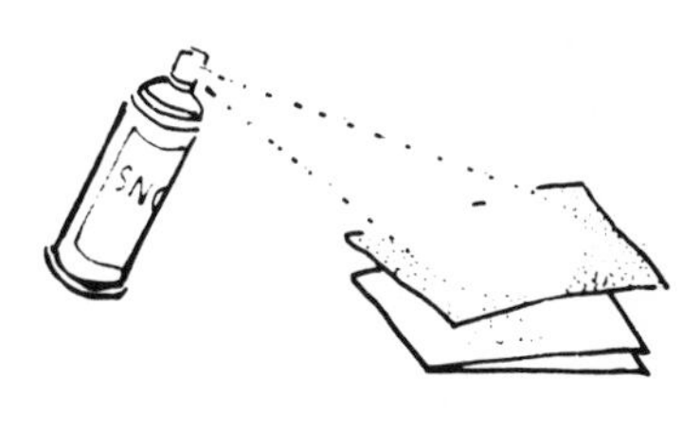

177. *Lay the stencil over a piece of paper and spray the page lightly with canned snow. Let it dry then remove.*

178. *You can also spatter paint with a toothbrush.*

Materials for a Found Object Stencil Print

Old nuts and bolts, washers, old keys and key rings, paper clips, plastic forks or spoons — anything you find that strikes your fancy.
White or colored paper
A toothbrush
Small watercolor brush
Poster colors and saucers of water

Printing Stencils with Found Objects

On a fold of paper, arrange the things you have found. See if you can make a design of a face, a figure, a car, or a boat with them (Figure 179).

Using one color, spatter one portion of your design. Spatter another portion of the design with another color (Figure 180). Perhaps you will discover you can blend in a third color. When the paint is dry, carefully remove the objects which have made your design.

179. *Arrange some found objects on a fold of paper.*

180. *Spatter one portion of the design with one color; another section with another color.*

Materials for a Cut Stencil Print

Tracing paper or carbon paper
Frisket tape
Sharp pencils
Stencil paper
Thumbtacks
X-Acto knife or single-edged razor blade
Poster paints and water
Saucers
Stencil brushes and toothbrushes
Scrap cardboard
Paper or card stock for your cards

Making a Cut Stencil Print

For your first cut stencil, perhaps you should try something as simple as a sailboat. The shape of the hull rising out of the waves, the sail, and the mast are all easy shapes to draw and cut. You can either offset a tracing of your sketch onto the stencil paper (see Chapter 3), or use carbon paper to transfer your design (Figure 181). Place the shiny side of the carbon against the stencil paper, put your design on top, then follow the outline of your design with a sharp pencil, pressing down hard enough to leave a line of carbon on the stencil paper. Now place the stencil paper on scrap cardboard and cut out those portions of your design through which paint will be daubed or spattered (Figure 182).

Now secure your stencil to the cardboard with either a bit of frisket tape or thumbtacks as shown in Figure 183. (If the stencil moves you'll have an uneven edge on your design, so keep the stencil secure.) To paint, use short-bristled stencil brushes with very little paint. (If you use too much paint, it will smear and blot.) Daub the paint carefully with short, quick motions, or spatter the paint with the toothbrush as you did earlier. You might find you will want to blend several colors in a fine spatter as you did in making a stencil with found objects.

Sometimes one stencil can be repeated in different colors over a long card to make a pattern in repeat. The leaping bunnies shown in Figure 184 were made from one stencil of two bunnies, put down and spattered four times. Try some experiments like this!

Also, notice the stencil of the dancing figure shown in Figure 185. The cut-out pieces were reassembled like found objects. The head, trunk, legs, and arms can be made to take any position — and then spatter-printed. You might want to make half a dozen entirely different cards with the same pieces.

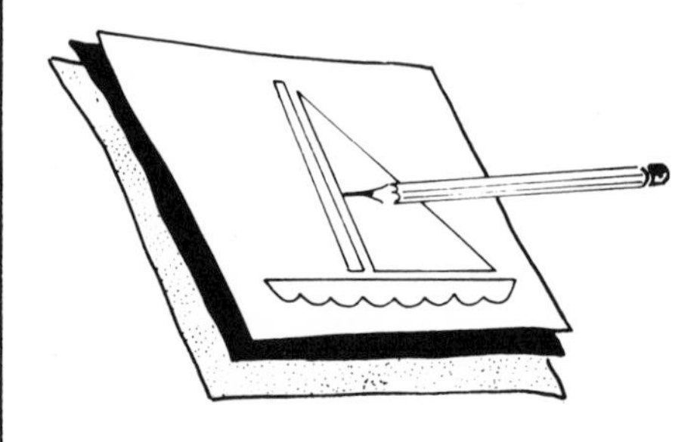

181. *Using pencil pressure through carbon paper, transfer the design to the stencil paper.*

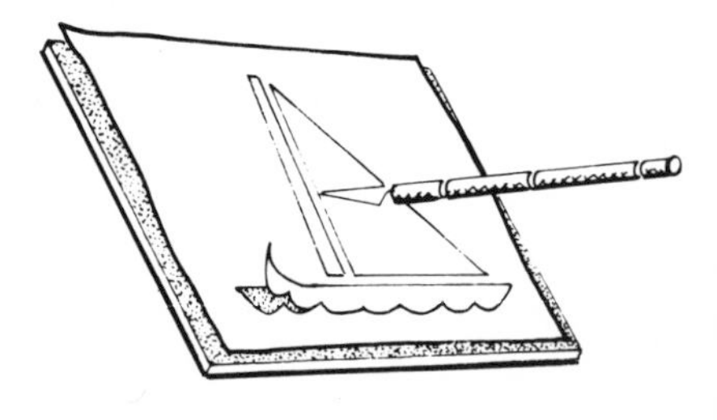

182. *Cut out your stencil against a cardboard to prevent marring.*

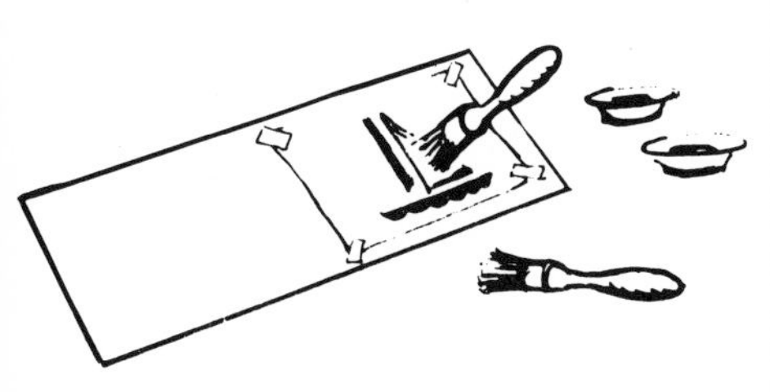

183. *Secure the stencil on all four sides to the card. Brush the color through with short-bristled stencil brushes and very little paint. Let the paint dry, and remove stencil.*

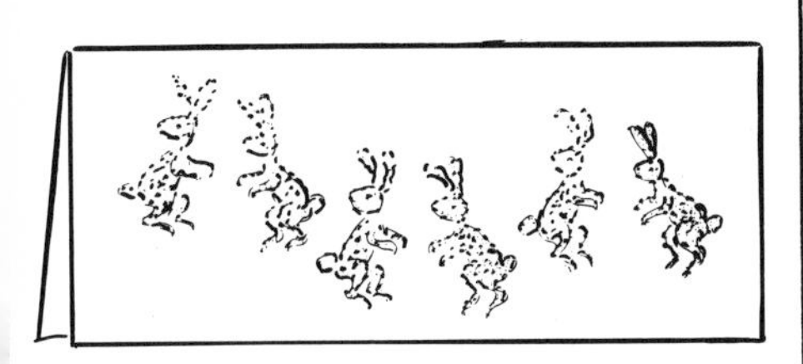

184. *This card was made with one stencil repeated three times.*

185. *These dancing figures consist of cut-out pieces of paper which were assembled in various positions and then spatter-printed.*

Pochoir

Pochoir, the French word for stencil, is a highly refined stencil method. Not only greeting cards, but costume plates, book illustrations, posters, and even very wet and loose watercolors are skillfully reproduced, using a series of clear acetate cut stencils, the best watercolor paints available, and big round stencil brushes. The stencils are notched in two corners for positioning or *registering* the colors.

I once had the opportunity to watch this work being done in a Paris shop. The outlines of a typical Montmartre street scene had been printed, by machine offset, in a light gray ink on sheets of watercolor paper. These printed sheets were quickly passed down a long table from one girl to the next; each one deftly brushed one or two colors through her particular stencil. The finished product was strikingly like the original painting shown to me. Let's try reproducing a watercolor or gouache sketch using clear acetate stencils as they do in France.

Materials for Pochoir

Sketch pad and pencils
Sheets of clear acetate the thickness of stencil paper
Pencils
Sharp mat knife or X-Acto knife
Watercolors and saucers
Big, round stencil brushes and inking wads of cloth
Talcum powder
Scrap cardboard and clean cloths
Paper or card stock

Printing the Pochoir

Prepare your watercolor sketch, keeping in mind the fact that a long, continuous line or cross-hatching — such as the figure eight shown in Figure 186 — will need two or more stencils. (Remember, without the ties, the entire design would drop through the stencil as described in regard to the letter *P* in Figure 173).

On a sheet of clear acetate — a plastic sheet that is similar to celluloid but is actually non-flammable cellulose acetate — slightly larger than the size of your card, "pounce" or rub the surface with talcum and a cloth; this will give "tooth" to the acetate. Notch two corners of the acetate and place it over your watercolor sketch, fastening the acetate in place with a bit of frisket tape (Figure 188). Outline all of one color with a pen line (Figure 189).

Now place this fresh acetate over your watercolor sketch again, fastening down with frisket tape, and outline and cut out another color, or make a stencil that will overlap the ties of the first color.

Notch and position as many stencils as you will need, cutting holes only for specific colors and tones. Let us say you have made eight clear acetate stencils, and are now ready to print. Place and fasten the first stencil over a sheet of fresh card stock, and brush or daub in the first color with paint that is not too wet (Figure 192). Allow the paint to dry. Now remove the first stencil and position and fasten the second clear acetate stencil, and carefully apply the next color. Continue with all of the stencils until you have reproduced your original watercolor. To save time, and if you can, you might paint your original watercolor

Next, remove the acetate from the watercolor sketch; place it on cardboard, and, with an X-Acto knife, cut out the areas you have outlined (Figure 190). Remove the acetate stencil from the cardboard. Place a fresh piece of acetate the same size over the acetate, tracing the position of the notches. Cut the notches (Figure 191). four times so that each stencil will cover four cards at a time. This will save you much time in printing.

This is a not-very-difficult method of graphic reproduction, which — with a little patience and care — can give you some really beautiful cards.

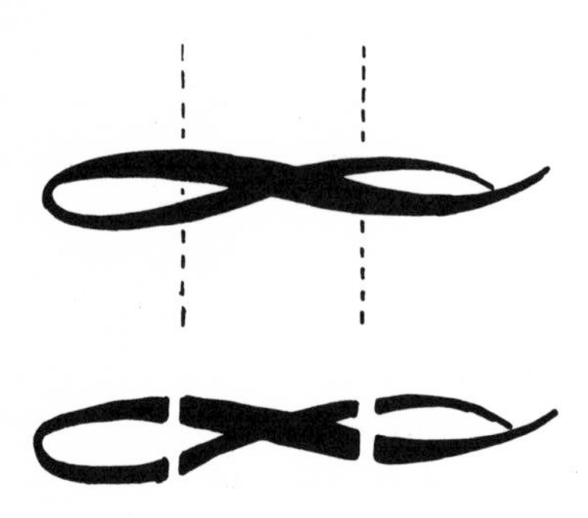

186. *In order to make this continuous line for a figure eight, three different stencils are needed. Any continuous lines or cross-hatching will require two or more stencils.*

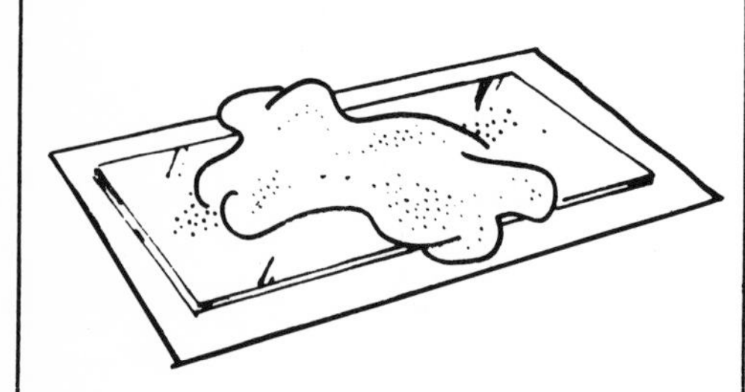

187. *Rub the surface of a sheet of clear acetate with talcum and cloth to give a "tooth" to the acetate.*

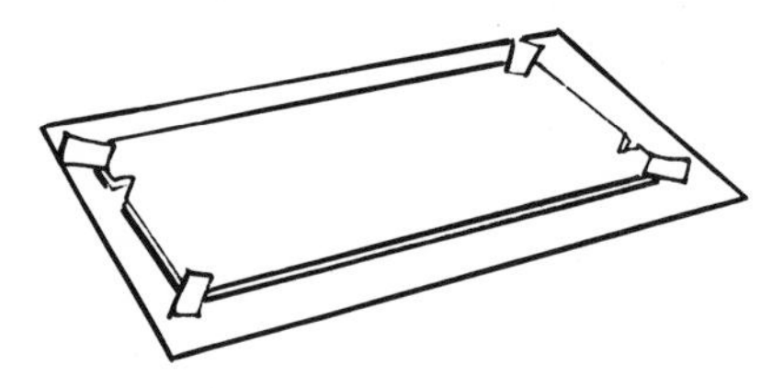

188. *Cut notches on the acetate — for color registration — and fasten down the sheet over the watercolor. Note the position of the notches on the watercolor in this sketch.*

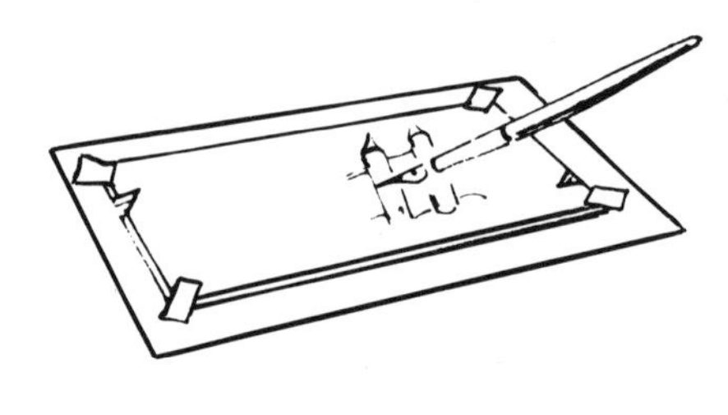

189. *Outline the areas of one color with a pen line.*

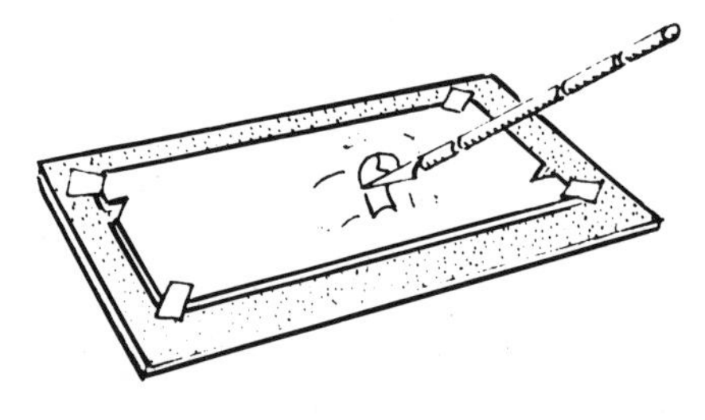

190. *Remove acetate, place it on a cardboard, and cut out the outlined areas with a knife.*

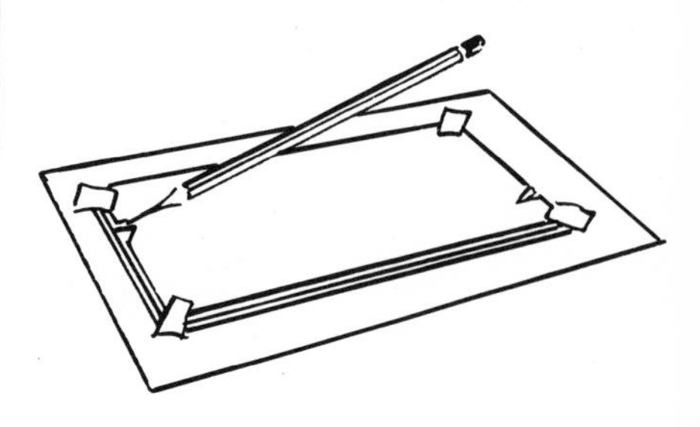

191. *For a second color, place a fresh sheet of acetate over the old sheet of acetate, and match the position of the notches. Cut out the notches.*

192. *Over a clean sheet of card stock, stencil with a not-too-wet dabber.*

193. *You can also stencil with the flat, round stencil brush.*

A simple, broad design — such as this one — is very appropriate for stencil work. This card involved the use of three stencils. By Niels Frederiksen.

By overlapping the color in this stencil print, interesting variations were obtained. By Niels Frederiksen.

An evergreen twig was used as a stencil for this card. Canned snow, sprayed over the foliage, produced a whispy silhouette effect. By John Carlis.

This is a one-color stencil print, with details added later by hand. By Niels Frederiksen.

11

Silk Screen

A silk screen is another kind of stencil. A piece of paper or film is glued down on a tightly stretched mesh of silk or organdy. The paper or film is the mask. The paint is forced through the areas of the mask that are cut. Because the silk screen is meshed, "ties" are unnecessary.

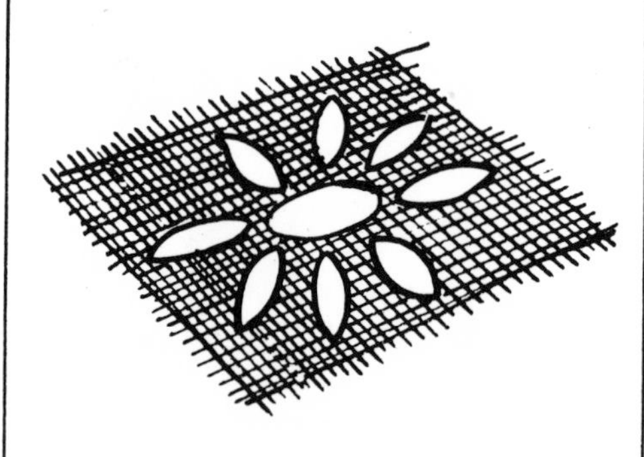

194. *Diagram of a cut-out stencil glued to a mesh, through which paint is forced.*

Homemade Silk Screen

Actually, you should start to silk screen with the basic kit prepared for beginners, sold by art suppliers. But if you have just finished dinner and the nearest art supply store is too far away, or if it's eight o'clock Saturday night and all the stores are closed, and you're anxious to make your very first screen print, perhaps I can help you make those 25 or 50 copies you need.

Materials for Homemade Silk Screen

Sketch pad
Pencils
Glue: LePage's, Sobo, or Elmer's
Board, about 15″ x 20″ (several thicknesses of cardboard will do)
Picture frame with simple molding (about 8″ x 10″)
Piece of organdy, milliners' crinoline, open-meshed silk, or a wide meshed silk stocking
Surgical or adhesive tape
Staple gun or hammer and tacks
Scissors, single-edged razor blades, or an X-Acto knife
Clean-up rags
Nail brush or toothbrush
One or two sheets of heavy brown Kraft paper (about 12″ x 15″), or one big piece of wrapping paper (about 20″ x 25″)
Shellac, if you have it, or some nail polish, any color
Ticket punch (optional)
Cornstarch (or a small box of prepared pudding with a cornstarch base)
Poster color, or watercolors in pans, or pure food color
Some short lengths of stiff cardboard (about 2″ x 4″)
Double boiler
Construction paper or any fairly heavy paper (plain gift wrapping or typewriter paper will do for trials)
Wax paper

Making the Screen

First reach for your picture frame. Remove the glass and small tacks from the frame. Stretching your piece of heavy crinoline or silk tightly, fasten it to the back of the frame with an office stapler, tacks, or glue (Figure 195).

Now cut up four strips of the heavy paper, 2″ wide, shellac them, and fasten them down all around the edge of the frame, leaving an opening in the middle of about 4″ x 6″ for your card print (Figure 196). The paper should be tightly sealed to the screen so that no ink will be able to seep through. You can use glue instead of shellac, sealing the inside edge of the paper with a line of nail polish. Now, with your surgical or adhesive tape, hinge one side of the frame down to the 15″ x 20″ board (Figure 197).

Applying the Design

Fold small pieces of the brown paper in two, and cut them into abstract decorative shapes, punching here and there with a ticket punch, if you have one (Figure 198). Shuffle around the pieces of cut paper on the screen until you've arranged a design that pleases you. Then carefully fasten each piece down on the crinoline, using shellac or nail polish (not glue, since you will later want to wash and scrub out this screen with water). Don't forget to fasten down some of the punched or cut-out dots as well, so that no ink will blur these openings.

Preparing the "Ink"

In a double boiler, put 2 tablespoonfuls of cornstarch in 1½ cups of water and bring to a boil. Stir, and when the mixture reaches the consistency of custard, turn off the flame. Take out ½ cup of the mix and keep it separate. Now add ½ teaspoon of poster color or several drops of watercolor or food coloring to the cornstarch in the pan, and add a different color to the mix in the cup. Stir the solution with a fork, adding more color as you need it. Make one of the colors bright, and one dark, remembering that a *light*, a *dark*, and a *bright* is a safe guide for an interesting color scheme. (Your paper will be the light.)

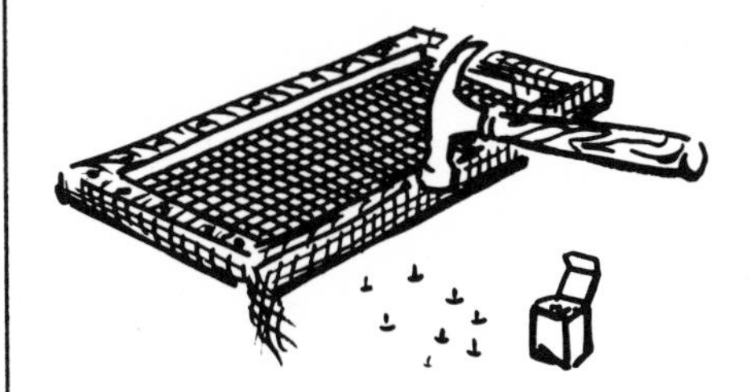

195. *After removing the glass and small tacks from a picture frame, stretch a piece of crinoline or silk tightly over the frame. Fasten the crinoline with tacks, stapler, or glue.*

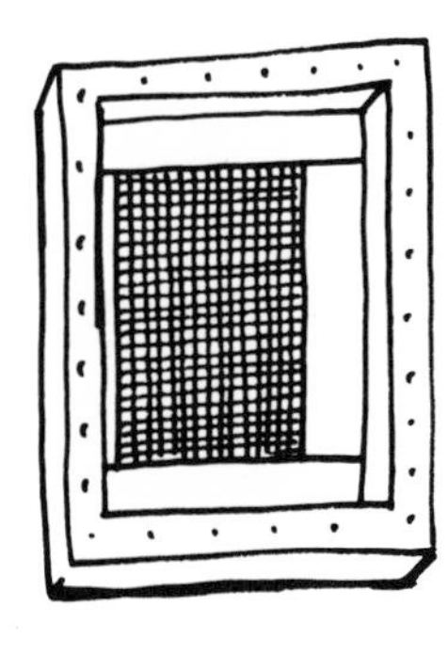

196. *Shellac down four strips of 2″ wide heavy paper along the edges, leaving an opening in the center of the crinoline about 4″ x 6″.*

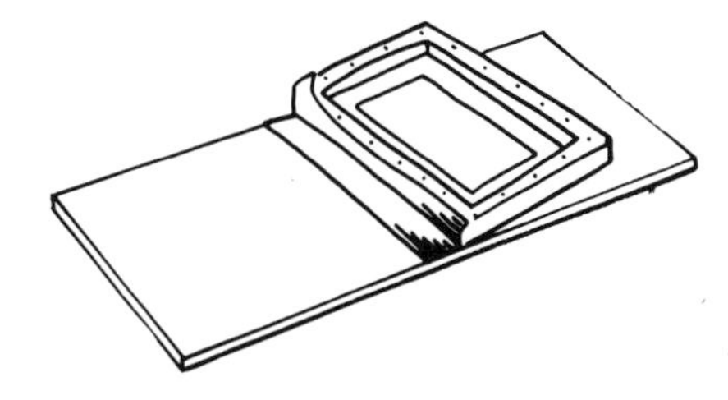

197. *With the surgical or adhesive tape, hinge one side of the frame down to a 15″×20″ board.*

198. *Cut folded pieces of brown paper into abstract shapes.*

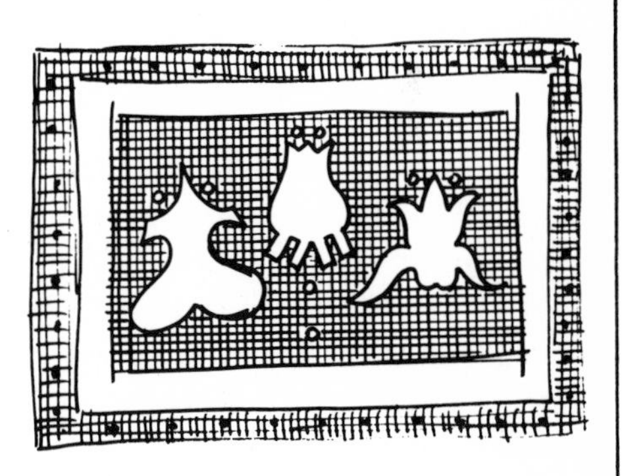

199. *After arranging a design of the paper cut-outs, fasten them down on the screen with shellac or nail polish.*

200. *Prepare the "ink." Put 2 tablespoonfuls of cornstarch and 2 tablespoons of flour in 1½ cups of water in a double boiler. Add coloring and bring to boil.*

The Printing Procedure

Your frame, with the design applied to the stretched crinoline or silk stocking, is hinged to the board. Lift up the unhinged side of the frame, and place a clean sheet of paper underneath the screen (Figure 201). Put the frame down against the paper.

Drop a couple of tablespoonfuls of your colored cornstarch mix along the inside edge of the frame (Figure 202). Now take one of the short lengths of stiff cardboard and quickly draw the "ink" mix across those portions of the crinoline or silk which were not masked by pieces of stuck-down paper (Figure 203). Lift the screen, remove the print, and repeat the operation. Interesting effects can be achieved by dropping a bit of the second color at either side of the screen or in the center of the design.

When these sheets have set for about ten minutes, interleave them between sheets of wax paper, and place a weight — such as a telephone directory — over the pile of sheets. (You have to weight cards printed with this "ink" because cornstarch has a tendency to buckle as it dries.)

Washing Up

Lift the screen and rub on both sides with wet rags to remove any excess ink (Figure 205). Gently scrub any stubborn areas with the nail brush or toothbrush; be careful not to scrub away any bits of the shellacked-down pieces of paper. Next, pat the screen dry with cloths and set it aside in a warm place where it will stretch taut again. Rest the screen frame on a 2" wide strip of cardboard in order to keep it away from the board so that the air can dry it.

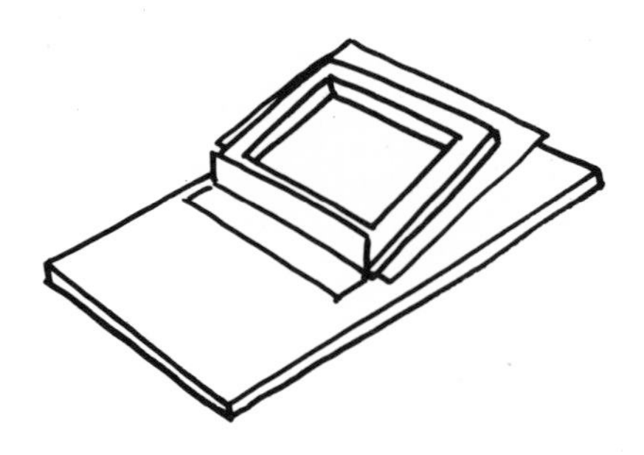

201. *Place a clean sheet of paper beneath the frame.*

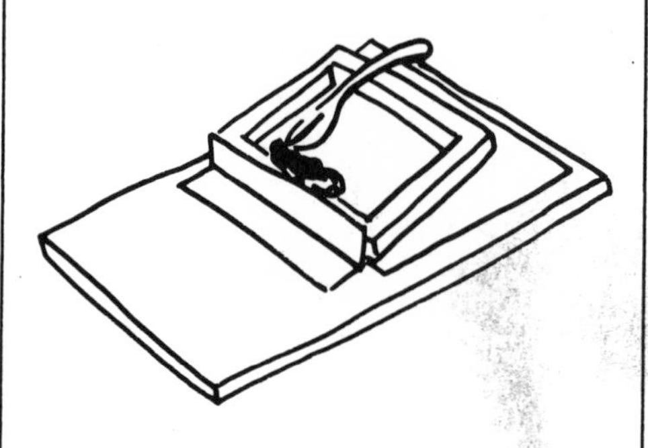

202. *Spoon some of the cornstarch "ink" into the frame edge.*

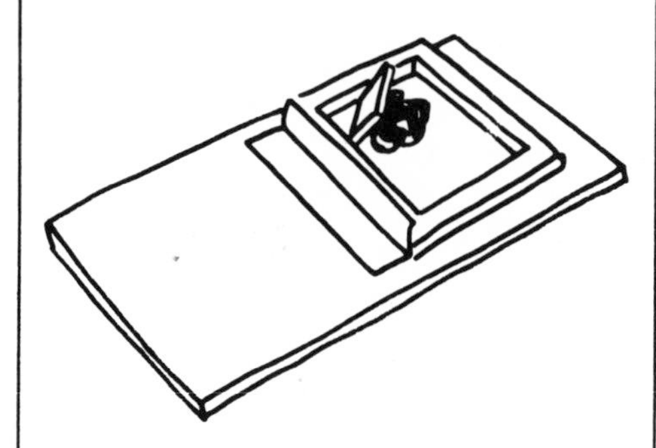

203. *Draw the "ink" across the design and through the mesh with a squeegee.*

204. *Lift up the screen and remove the print from the frame.*

205. *Clean the screen by rubbing both sides with wet cloths. Gently scrub stubborn areas with a brush.*

More Advanced Silk Screening

Silk screening — on a larger and more efficient scale than the homemade screens just described — is an enormously popular technique for making greeting cards. Let's try making a more advanced print: two greeting cards at one time, in several colors, using the *tusche and glue method.*

Materials for Silk Screens

From your art supplier, Sears-Roebuck, or Montgomery Ward, order a standard silk screen set (about $15.00) which will include: printing frame with hinge bar (a strip of wood which allows you to adjust the screen to the thickness of your paper or cardboard); jig with metal hinges; masking tape; wood and rubber squeegees; silk screen process inks; lacquer filler; transparent base; lacquer thinner; lacquer; block out dope; water soluble film; mixing paddles; stencil cutting knife.

To these items add:

Pencils
Sketch pad
LePage's Glue
Tusche
Small bottle of glycerine
Litho crayons and China marking pencils
Brushes
Scrap 1″ x 1″ wood strips, 4″ or 5″ long
Cellophane tape
Some big empty coffee tins for rags
Clean-up rags

Preparing the Master Sketch

Make color renderings of two designs, measuring 3½″ x 5″ each, using three or four colors in each. Avoid detail; use big rather than small color areas, and keep the outlines simple. Prepare these sketches on one sheet of paper with 1″ separating the two designs — to measure 5″ x 8″ on a 7″ x 10″ sheet; that is, with a 1″ margin all around (see Figure 206).

Masking the Margins

The frame in your printing set will measure 9″ x 12″ and will be already hinged to a board and stretched with silk. Now you will want to mask the margins on the screen, leaving a 5″ x 8″ open area in the middle for your two designs, which will be separated by a 1″ strip for the two areas of 3½″ x 5″. With Scotch tape, fasten your master sketch to the board beneath the screen, allowing a margin of 2″ all around the screen's printing area of 9″ x 12″. Glue register marks of thin cardboard to the board (Figure 207 and 208). Register marks will ensure your print always being in the same position on the paper — of prime importance when you print in more than one color. Lower the screen over the sketch — see Figure 209 — and with a soft pencil and a ruler, outline on the silk the two printing areas of 3½″ x 5″. This kind of screen will allow you to print two little pictures at the same time.

Now remove the screen from its hinges (take out the pins) and place the screen on four wood strips of 1″ x 1″ (Figure 210). Place a strip of cellophane tape *inside* the pencil outlines to keep the area open and to maintain straight edges in your design area. Now paint or squeegee a border of lacquer filler to mask and fill the 1″ center dividing strip (Figure 211). What you will have now is a screen with two windows, 3½″ x 5″; the designs will

206. *Make two designs, measuring 3½″×5″ each on a sheet of paper. Use three or four colors in each. Each design should have a 1″ margin.*

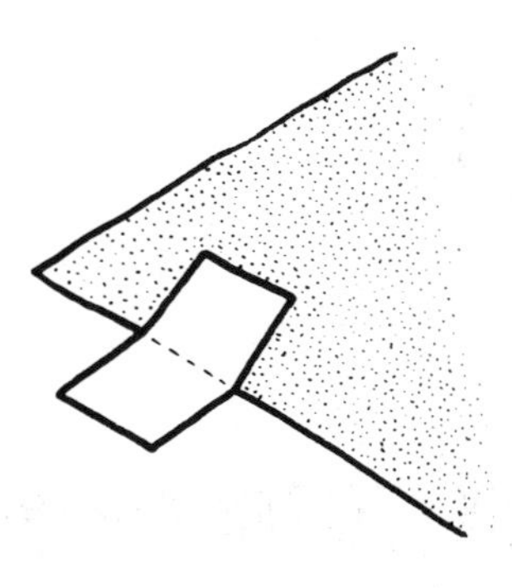

207. *Here is a close-up of the register marks: thin cardboard, half of which is bent to stop the paper, and half glued to the board.*

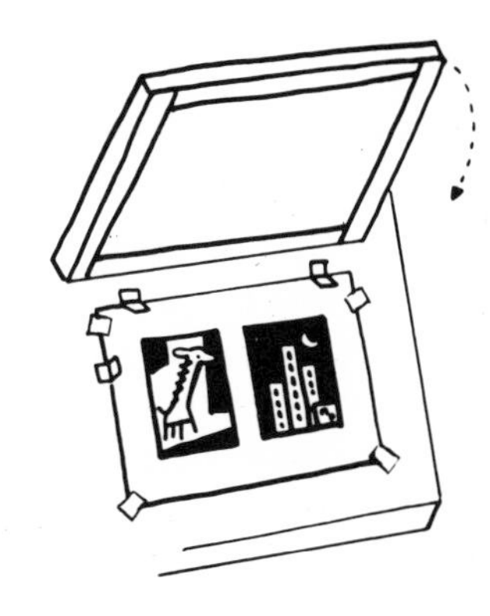

208. *Slip the master sketch under the screen; push the paper against the register marks and fasten down the sketch with four pieces of Scotch tape.*

fit in these windows; the rest will be masked out. Turn screen over. Repeat opaquing with lacquer on the reverse side of the screen (Figure 212). When dry, the screen will be even more transparent, and drum tight. Further seal the edges of the frame with lengths of gummed tape or with coats of lacquer filler. Do this carefully so that you seal the screen completely.

Painting With Tusche

Let us say your designs use red, yellow, light blue, and a navy blue. Looking through the silk, you will now paint with tusche wherever there is red in your design. Tusche, a black, greasy ink, is liquid lithographic crayon. Use the tusche thick, rather than thin. (You may have to pour some in a saucer and let it evaporate if it is too watery.) Lift up a corner of the screen, and let it rest on some match books, so that the screen is slightly raised away from the master sketch and the tusche will not drip onto it (Figure 214). Brush the tusche only *onto* the surface of the silk, not through it. After you've painted in all the red areas of both your designs, set the screen aside to dry.

Blocking Out With Glue

Prepare a half a cup of solution, 60% LePage's Glue and 40% water. Raise the screen frame up on the 1″ x 1″ sticks. When the tusche is dry, pour some of the glue solution into the screen and quickly squeegee over the whole area, including the areas where the tusche has been applied (Figure 215). Scoop up any excess glue solution, and then set the screen aside to dry. You can speed up the drying by fanning.

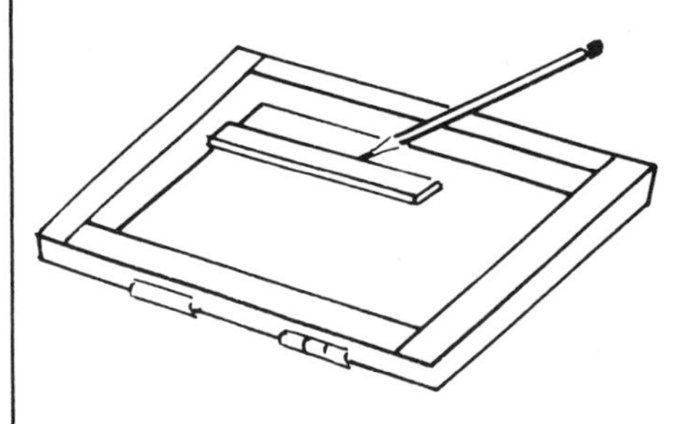

209. *Lower the screen and outline the two printing areas of 3½″×5″, using a soft pencil and a ruler.*

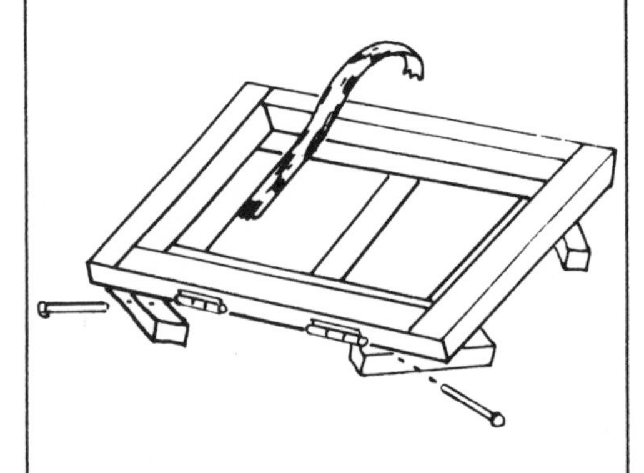

210. *Remove the screen from its hinges — by taking out the pins — and place it on four pieces of wood. Place strips of cellophane tape inside the pencil lines.*

211. *Fill the border of the screen with lacquer in order to opaque the border so it will not print.*

212. *Turn the screen over, and repeat opaquing operation on reverse side of screen.*

213. *Completed opaquing on reverse side with cellophane strips removed.*

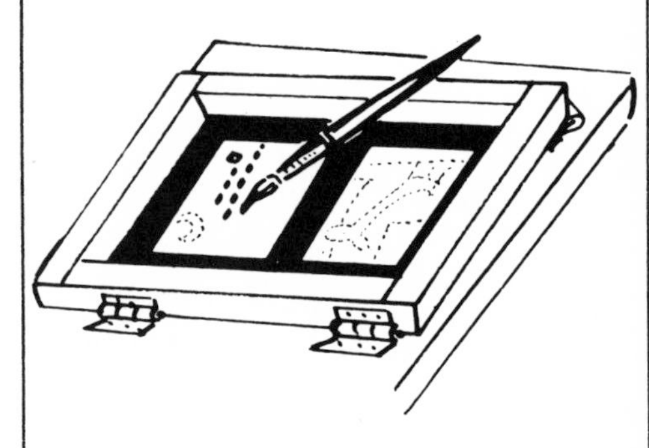

214. *Put the screen back on its hinges. Lift up a corner of the screen so that it is not touching the sketch. Brush the tusche onto the surface of the silk.*

215. *Raise the screen frame on the wooden sticks. With a glue solution (60% LePage's Glue and 40% water) pour the glue solution into the frame, on top of the dry tusche.*

216. *Place some newspapers under the frame and pour kerosene onto the screen. Wash out the tusche — but not the glue — by rubbing the kerosene in with rags throughout.*

217. *Mix up the ink: combine the concentrated ink with some of the transparent base, stirring the solution with a wooden paddle.*

Washing Out the Tusche

Place some newspapers under the frame, and pour a little kerosene onto the screen. By gently rubbing the kerosene on the screen (with cloths), you will wash out the areas of tusche and the glue will remain as a mask in all the other areas of the screen (Figure 216). Be sure to put the oily rags in a covered metal can or throw them away with the oily newspaper at once.

Printing the Silk Screen

Your red ink in the can will be too thick. Put some in an empty can and mix in some of the transparent base, stirring with a wooden paddle. More base makes your color more transparent. The consistency of very soft butter would be about right for these two small prints.

Now raise your screen and place a sheet of paper against the cardboard register guides or stops (Figure 218). Lower the screen, and put some of the mixed red ink along the edge of your screen. Squeegee the ink across the designs with your rubber squeegee or with a stiff piece of cardboard, forcing the ink through the openings on the screen (Figure 219). Lift the screen, and remove the printed sheet. Print the red on all of the cards.

Printing the Other Colors

After you've printed the red areas on all the cards, clean up the screen. Place some newspapers under the frame and, with pieces of cardboard, remove all the remaining red ink from the screen. Changing the newspapers, pour some kerosene into the frame, cleaning carefully with rags. When the frame is dry, wash out the glue with warm water and clean cloths. Briskly rub a nailbrush or a toothbrush over the screen to remove any stubborn spots of glue. When the screen is clean and dry, lift it again, position your design, and paint in all of the next color, the yellow, using the liquid tusche. Proceed as you did with the first color.

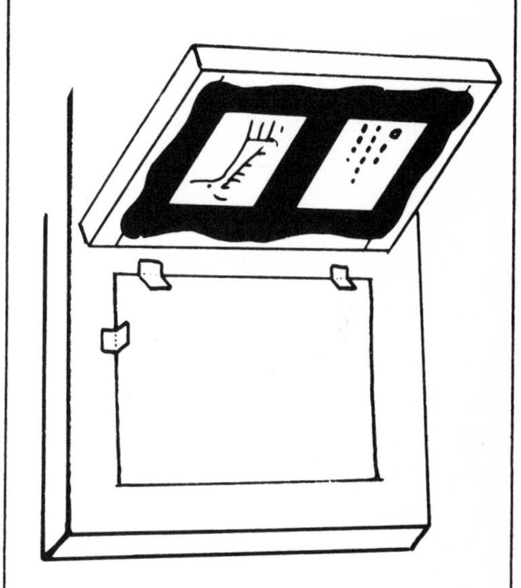

218. *Raise the screen and place a sheet of paper against the register guides.*

219. *Lower the screen, drop some ink along the frame and squeegee the ink across the design, forcing the ink through the openings on the screen.*

Drying and Mounting Prints

To dry prints, you can hang them on a line with snap clothespins (Figure 220) or you can spread them out over a long table. For drying large quantities, a built-up stack of cardboards and ½" x 1" x 24" (or whatever length you prefer) sticks—forming a rack arrangement—is a space saver. (See Figure 221.)

To mount the prints, you can either tip them inside cut-out openings of French folds (as shown in Figure 222) or you can attach them to borders of colored or metallic papers.

Variations on Screen Printing

You can transfer a rubbing to a silk screen and print the rubbing by the tusche and glue method. Moreover, silk screens can be stamp printed and blotted with tusche, and it is not inconceivable that a silk screened greeting card could successfully combine potato prints or linocuts, blots and rubbings. Techniques are only a means to an end, and a mixed method may express a particular idea better than any *one* method of graphic reproduction.

220. *Cards can be hung on a clothesline to dry.*

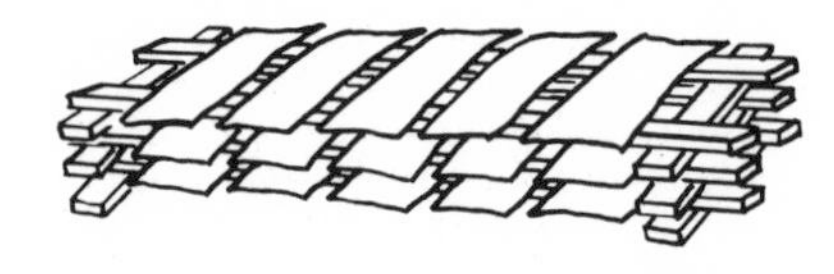

221. *Cards can be stacked on 2' lengths of sticks which have been arranged to form a rack.*

222. *To mount the prints, you can place them inside the cut-out face of a French fold or you can tip them onto borders of colored or metallic papers.*

This was a homemade silk screen. Notice how the coarse screen adds a pleasant texture to the over-all design. By John Carlis.

Using the symbols Alpha, Omega, Birth, Christ, the artist created a strong design for this two-color silk screen. By Julio Micheli, Jr.

The artist used only three colors in this card. The head of the scarlet red dove overlaps the orange sun, creating an interesting design element within the drawing. By Shosha.

A silk screen print can be made on virtually any surface. Here the card was silk screened on a piece of tri-toned fabric. The cloth was then mounted on a contrasting card stock. By Calister Simpson.

Here the artist printed a two-color silk screen in two transparent colors. He used the same stencil for each color, but moved the register tabs about ⅜" so that the colors overlapped slightly, adding what appears to be a third color. By Julio Micheli, Jr.

This silk screen involved the use of five colors, both transparent and opaque. To create a sense of low relief in the figures of the three wise men, the register tabs were moved slightly to a new position. The slight mis-register created a desirable effect. By Julio Micheli, Jr.

No elaborate design is necessary to make a card really imaginative. The three crowns are printed in a bright green, blue, and red. By Ivan Chermayeff.

An Indian fabric inspired the design of this silk screen Christmas card. By Karen Leonard.

12

Printing with Light

There are a variety of ways to print with light and I will describe three in this chapter: the Xerox print, the blueprint, the photogram.

The Xerox Print

The Xerox machine, which you can find nowadays in most offices or stationery stores — and a new model, which costs less than a typewriter, may soon be seen in homes as well — is one of the most simple ways of printing with light.

Materials for Xerox Greeting Cards

White typewriter paper
Pen ink or black felt tipped pen
Sharp pencils
Eraser
Ruler
Xerox machine
Magic Markers

Printing Procedure

With a ruler and a light pencil line, divide a sheet of typewriter paper in half each way, so that you have four rectangles measuring 4¼″ x 5½″ (Figure 223). Then, with the ruler and a light pencil line, draw a ¼″ border all around for trim, so you will have four rectangles measuring 3¾″ x 5″ each (Figure 224).

Now draw the same or a different design in each of the four rectangles with black pen and ink (Figure 225). You can use some pencil shading in the design if you like (though don't try for too much tonal gradation or you'll be disappointed.) You can also do as much lettering as you please. Leave some open areas for Magic Marker coloring. For a couple of dozen cards, place your drawing with the special printing paper in the machine six times. Add Magic Marker coloring to your designs. Cut the cards apart, and mount them on folds of colored paper.

Materials for Blueprint Cards

Large sheets of transparent tracing paper (the 19″ x 24″ Lexington tracing pad is a good one)
Pen and black ink or black felt tipped pen
Sharp pencils
Eraser
Ruler
Single-edged razor blade or an X-Acto knife
Clear cellophane tape
Paper doilies
Scissors
Black paper
Elmer's Glue-All
Zip-a-tone textures
Alphabets

Making Blueprint Cards

With your ruler and a light pencil, draw off four French fold cards on a sheet of 19″ x 24″ tracing paper. (That is, divide the sheet into four areas of 9½″ x 12″ each.) Now, with this 19″ x 24″ sheet of paper in front of you, divide each 9½″ x 12″ area into four again, giving you smaller areas of 4¾″ x 6″ for your design (Figure 228).

Use a different technique in each of the four designs: draw one entirely with pencil and ink; use black paper cut-outs tipped to the tracing paper by pinpoints of Elmer's Glue-All and overlays of strips of cellophane tape for another design; for the third design, make a pattern of cut apart lace paper doilies, again tipped to the tracing paper with the smallest amount of

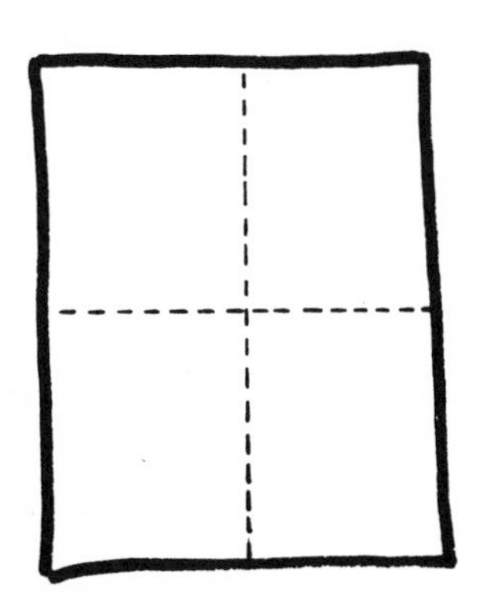

223. *Divide a sheet of typewriter paper into half each way. Each rectangle measures* $4\frac{1}{4}'' \times 5\frac{1}{2}''$.

224. *Draw a* $\frac{1}{2}''$ *border all around the sheet. (Now each rectangle is* $3\frac{3}{4}'' \times 5''$.*)*

225. *In each of the rectangles, draw pen and ink designs.*

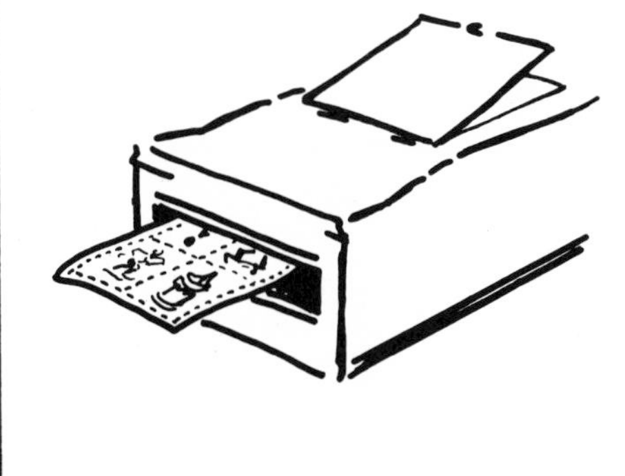

226. *Run the drawings through the Xerox machine.*

227. *Color in open areas with a Magic Marker of any tint.*

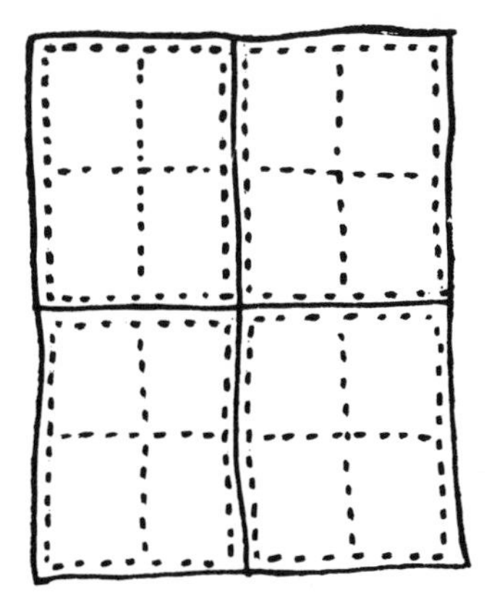

228. *Divide a* $19'' \times 24''$ *sheet of tracing paper into quarters. Then divide each quarter into fours again. These will be four French fold cards.*

229. *Draw one design in pencil and pen and ink.*

230. *Draw another design in pencil, pen and ink, with bits of paper doilies.*

231. *Using cut black paper and strips of cellophane tape, you can make a "patched up heart."*

Elmer's Glue-All. Make a border of cellophane tape and strips of scrap tracing paper for a fourth design (Figures 229-232). Turn your sheet upside down and letter your greeting in the lower right hand corners of the $9^{1}{}_{2}$″ x 12″ rectangles (Figure 233).

Take this sheet to a blueprinter and order two copies printed. You will be pleasantly surprised (by the variation in tones of blue and white the light creates shining through the various opacities. Make any changes you think necessary, and order more copies printed. Cut each print into four French fold cards, or skip writing the message and have blueprints made of only the designs. Then you can tip each design onto folds of contrasting colors of paper.

Insteaa of blueprints, you can order brownprints. With brownprints you can spike the range of beiges to deep cocoa tones, using Magic Marker touches of apricot, pumpkin, gold, lime, or aqua! Two or three sheets of blue- or brownprints made from extra large sheets of tracing paper might easily provide you with all the greetings you will need — once they are cut apart and mounted. If you have just moved into a brand new house or apartment, you might want to make an announcement card from a blueprint, imitating an architectural drawing and lettering. It might be fun to send this to all those friends who held your hand while you were being "Mr. and Mrs. Blanding" or while you were apartment hunting.

Blueprints with a solid blue background have recently been superseded by a newer process that prints a blue or a black line on a white background, so the *solid* background of blue may not be possible much longer. Be aware of this when you select a blueprinter.

232. *Create a dancing figure with cellophane tape, cut paper, and paper lace to give lively translucent effects.*

233. *Place each design in the lower right hand corners of each original 9½″×11″ rectangle. Turn the sheet upside down and write in the greeting in the lower right hand corners.*

234. *In the blueprint, everything that had been black in your design will now be white against blue. To the blue and white, you can add a dash of Magic Marker color.*

235. *Cut apart the four designs to make four French fold cards.*

Photogram Greeting Cards

Essentially, photograms are a kind of photography without a camera. Pictures made with the sun or with a light bulb exposed on photographic paper are called photograms. These are distinguished by a wide range of soft gray tones and sharp blacks and whites; a gradation of gray into a dense black. You can obtain a soft, blurry quality, or a sharp pattern which is as crisp as a cobweb. For example, confetti with some threads of fine silk and fuzzy wool, sprinkled on the photoprint paper, will have a definition very few artists have been able to achieve with pencils or paint, and very different from any of the effects we have tried so far in this book.

Materials for Photograms

An improvised darkroom: any space that will allow you to stand in front of a table, from which light can be shut out
Red light bulb or flashlight with red glass or red cellophane
Three flat glass or enamel dishes, about 8″ x 10″
Clean, slick surface (glass, tin, or enamel), about 8″ x 10″
Pack of photoprint paper
Photo developer
Photo fixer
Acetic acid
Glass or porcelain rod
Running water or a gallon jug of water
Sheet of glass (8″ x 10″)
Pencil flashlight
Big flashlight
X-Acto knife
Brass-edged ruler
Confetti, threads of silk and wool
Clear acetate with a "tooth" (8″ x 10″)
India ink and watercolor brush and pen
Sponge
Scissors
Paper of various opacities: tissue paper, tracing paper, bond, etc.
Any small objects of design that interest you: paper clips, charms, dried and pressed flowers, leaves, broken glass, alphabet soup letters, negatives of old snapshots, etc.

Setting up the Darkroom

First prepare the photographic chemicals (a procedure which can be done in daylight). Following the directions on the package, mix the developer with water in one of the three flat glass dishes. Again following the directions on the package, mix a glass dish of the hypo or photo fixer. Place a pan of clear water between these two, adding a drop of the acetic acid to the clear water. (This is called the *stop bath.*) Have your photoprint paper safely in its black paper envelope where you can reach for it easily while you are working with only the red light.

Preparing the Design

Place a piece of clear acetate—which has been rubbed with talcum and a cloth to give it a "tooth"—on top of the piece of glass. On the acetate, divide the 8″ x 10″ area into four 4″ x 5″ areas with a pen line. In one of the 4″ x 5″ areas, make a design with some bits of broken glass and some dried grasses. In another, make a design combining drawing (with brush or pen and ink) and confetti and threads of silk and wool. Perhaps you'll want to try some of these elements with a cut-up negative or some alphabet soup

236. *Prepare three pans of solutions: the developer, the stop bath, and the hypo.*

letters. Always keep in mind that you will be working with light and opacities, so in another area combine drawing and cut-outs of papers of various weights. Leave the last area blank.

Making the Print

Now turn off the white lights and be sure that the only light in the room comes from a red bulb or a flashlight covered with red cellophane. Carefully remove one sheet of photoprint paper from the envelope, and close the envelope. Now lift the designed acetate and glass, and slip the photograph paper underneath, the shiny emulsion side up (Figure 241). With your big flashlight, flash the page with white light for a second. Remember, the longer you expose the paper to the white light, the blacker it will become once it is developed. If you flash the penlight quickly in the blank 4″ x 5″ area, moving it in fast curves, zig-zags, or circles, you'll be painting dark lines with soft edges. Try the pen flashlight on other designs, too. (Naturally, you won't see the design on the paper until you develop the paper. The sheet will stay white until you place it in the developer. Then you'll see the design emerge!)

237. *Prepare acetate by rubbing some talcum powder on the surface to give it "tooth."*

238. *Place the clear acetate on top of a piece of glass.*

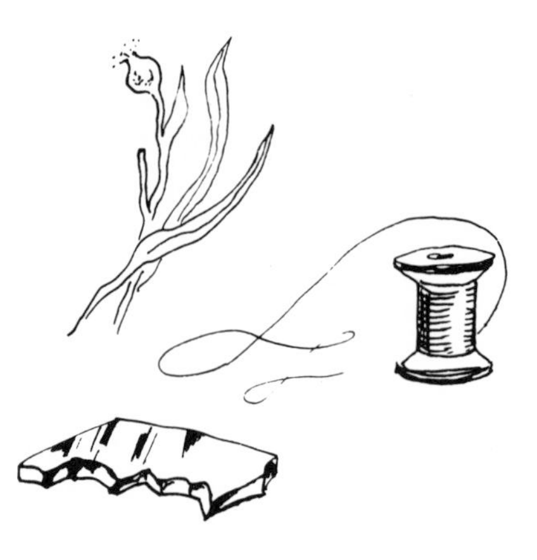

239. *Assemble various found objects.*

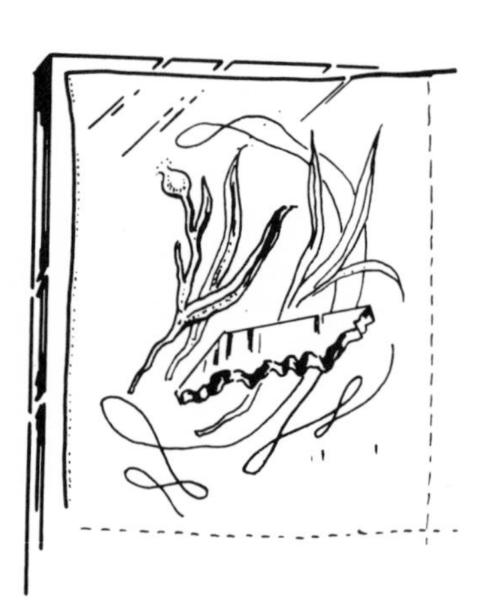

240. *Arrange the found objects on the clear acetate: broken glass, grasses, thread, etc.*

241. *After turning off all the white lights—leaving on only the red—slip a sheet of photographic paper under the sheet of glass, shiny emulsion side facing up.*

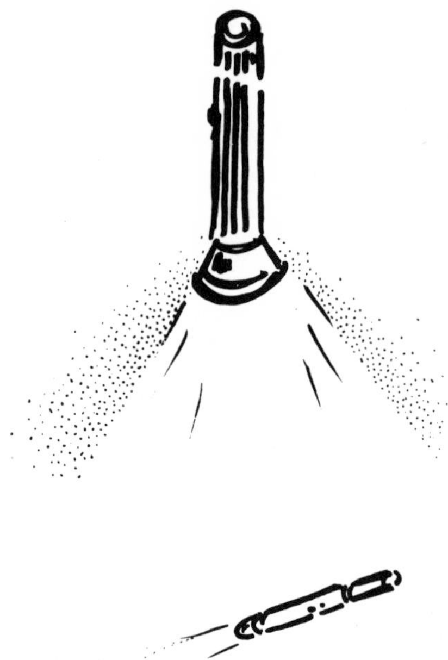

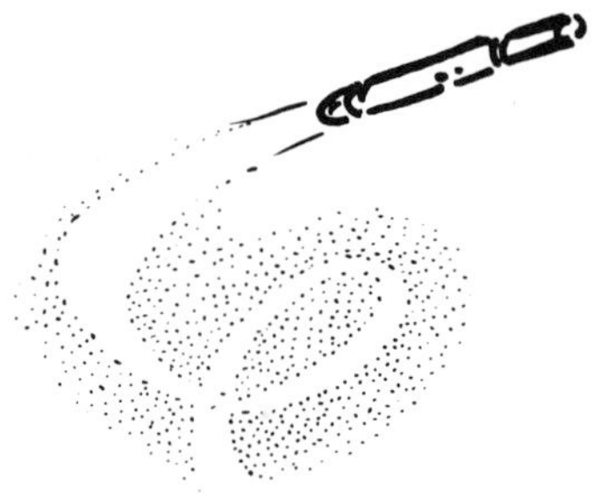

242. *Flash your white flashlight on the paper; a few rapid turns with the pen flashlight.*

Developing the Print

Lift off the glass and acetate and — without turning on the lights — place the photoprint paper in the pan of developer. Don't let the paper rise to the surface of the solution; poke it down thoroughly into the developer with a glass or porcelain rod. Watch your four little patterns take shape. As soon as you have some real blacks, remove the paper and plunge it into the middle pan of clear water. Rinse quickly in this pan, and then put the sheet into the pan of hypo to "fix" the developing. Let the prints stand in the hypo bath for a half hour. (Once the paper has been in the hypo a few minutes, you can turn on the lights again.) Next, rinse the paper thoroughly in running water for about a half hour, and place it on a slick surface — an enamel table top, for example — to dry. Press any remaining water out with your fingers and a sponge. If you are in your bathroom, you can press the prints around the inside walls of your tub, being sure they don't fall and curl up on the bottom of the tub.

When you study your card in the light, you might find it went too black. If so, go back into the darkroom and expose another sheet of paper to less light. Conversely, if the sheet is too gray, give the next one a bigger shot of white light.

You can also vary the technique. For example, try rolling the acetate gently away from the paper as you expose the sheet to light to get a different effect. You can also draw directly on the acetate with brush and ink, place the drawing over a sheet of paper, and expose it to light.

243. *Run the paper through the three pans of developer, rinse with water, and place on flat surface to dry.*

Mounting the Prints

When the sheet is dry, cut the four images apart and mount them on a fold of colored paper (Figure 243). You might want to add a touch of hand color — or maybe you prefer the richness of grays and the black and white contrasting with the mounting paper.

244. *Mount your photogram on a fold of colored paper.*

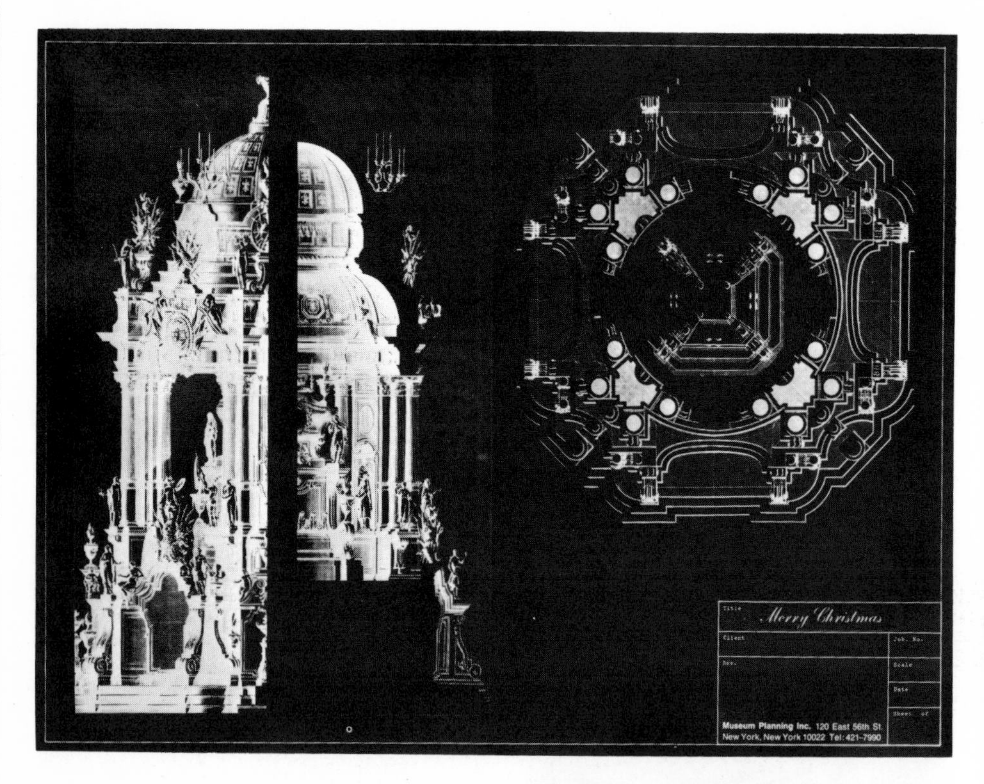

To symbolize his profession, this designer of museums produced a blueprint of an old architectural engraving. By William Harris.

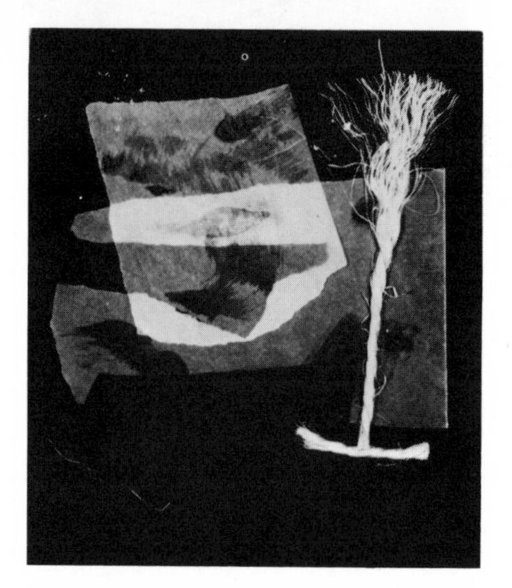

To make this photogram, the artist placed a piece of string, transparent paper, and gift wrapping paper under a sheet of glass. By John Carlis.

A plastic snowflake, laid over a wide mesh screen, provided the motif for this photogram Christmas card. By John Carlis.

A linear design, such as this one, can be Xeroxed and hand colored. By Joanna Mersereau.

The artist posed for this photograph, inserted a brief holiday message, and made photostats for his friends. By Nick Meglin.

Try taking a high contrast photograph, with sharp darks and lights, which you can Xerox or photostat for a greeting card. You'd be surprised how dramatic the effects can be. Jane, Amy, Tobe, and Ed Berkovitz.

This is a high contrast silhouette photograph, and something like this can be photostatted for Christmas cards. By Esther Bubley. Collection, Dione Guffey.

Children's art can be a charming motif for a card. This is a blueprint. By Jimmy West.

Although this may look like several Santa's doing handsprings, actually there are only two. The artist made an offset tracing several times, drew over the lines in ink and Xeroxed several for mailing. By Susan E. Meyer.

13

Gelatin Prints

The gelatin film duplicator, available from any office supplier for about $4.00, prints from 50 to 100 copies in as many as five different colors at one time! If you have ever sent out a last minute office notice or a PTA announcement, I'm sure you will remember how easy it is to print anything written, typed, drawn, or traced with this duplicator. Or perhaps you've tried to read a carelessly made and fuzzily purple typewritten menu at a lunch counter somewhere. *Clean* copies *are* quite possible, but a characteristic of this duplicating method is a certain softness — a quality which can be used to advantage in making your own greeting cards.

Materials for Gelatin Prints

Hectograph duplicator: available from your stationer or directly from the manufacturer, Mimeo Manufacturing Co., Inc. (see shopping guide). The gelatin compound comes in the following sizes: note size (no. 1906: $1.75); letter size (no. 1911: $2.00); legal size (no. 1914: $2.25).

Clear-Print Hecto inks (purple, blue, red, green, and black)
Carbon paper
Clear-Print Hecto pencils (purple, blue, red, green)
Sponge
Hand cleaning liquid
Construction paper in white or ivory tints
Ruler
Roll of waxed paper
X-Acto knife

Preparing the Master

Remove a master sheet from the package. Lift the carbon, and draw directly on the master with Hecto colored pencils — or type, write, trace, or draw on the master through the carbon (Figure 245). You can use several colored Hecto pencils or inks on the same master — just as you would on an original drawing. You can also make your drawing with Hecto colored pencils or inks on a sheet of construction paper or on any paper fairly heavy in weight. It will not be necessary to reverse any lettering. Remember to work on a smooth, hard surface.

Preparing the Gelatin Plate

Apply cool water to the surface of the gelatin with a sponge, allowing a minute for the water to penetrate (Figure 246). Blot up excess water with a sponge, and remove any further free moisture by applying a sheet or two of blank copy paper. No excess water should remain on the film surface. Place the master face down on the moistened gelatin, touching one end of the master to the gelatin film surface, and smoothing it into perfect contact (Figure 247). Smoothing the master into position ensures perfect transfers. Rub the back of the drawing lightly. Let it remain for about thirty seconds for a short run; three minutes for a longer run (50 to 100 copies). Carefully remove the master drawing and you're ready to print (Figure 248). You'll see your copy in reverse on the gelatin: this is your printing plate.

The Printing Procedure

Place your printing paper (any kind of paper is sufficient) over the gelatin; smooth it down with your fingers and, after waiting about thirty seconds, carefully lift off the paper, getting a good grip on one corner. (If the corner is dog-eared by your grip, it can be trimmed off later. Some patterns in three or four colors may need as much as five minutes for good copies. However, thirty seconds to a minute is usually sufficient.

Drying

Your prints will be slightly damp from the moistened gelatin. Slipsheet them between sheets of waxed paper and put them under a weight — a telephone directory will do nicely — so they will dry flat (Figure 251). An hour's drying time should be enough.

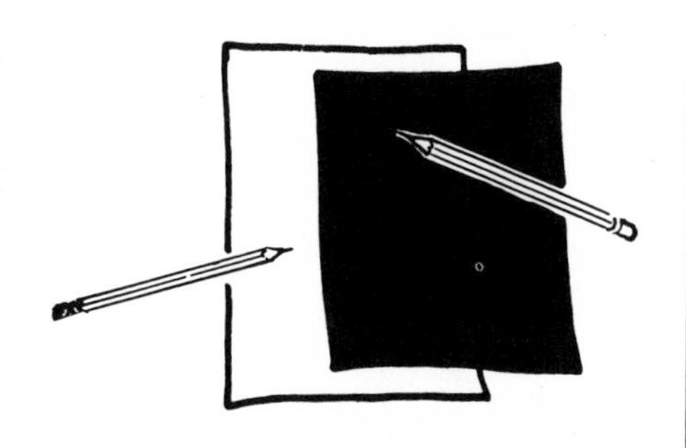

245. *Draw directly on the Hectograph master with the Hecto colored pencils or draw directly through the carbon.*

246. *Moisten the surface of the gelatin with a little cool water and a sponge.*

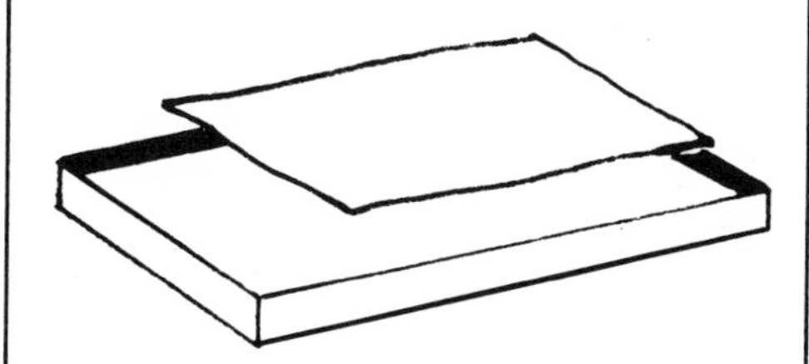

247. *Place the master face down on the gelatin.*

248. *Carefully lift off the master. Gelatin will now be your printing plate.*

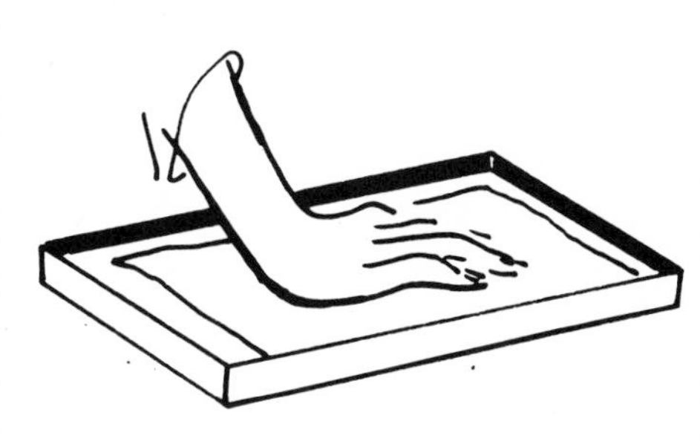

249. *Drop the printing paper over the gelatin and smooth down the sheet with your fingers.*

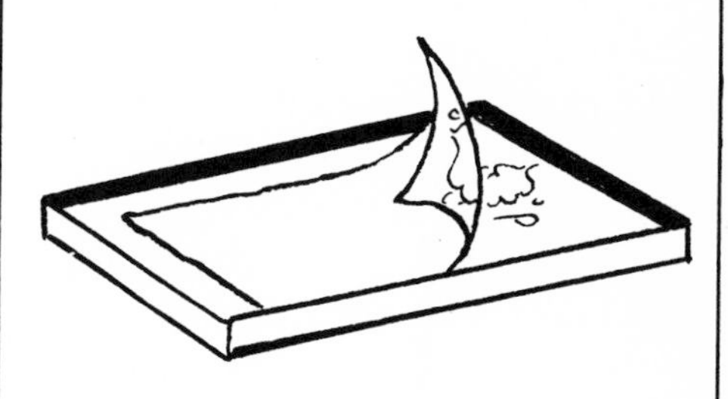

250. *Lift away the paper by getting a good grip on the corner.*

251. *Slipsheet the damp prints between sheets of waxed paper and put them under a weight to dry.*

Further Notes

The Hectograph will give you excellent facsimiles of drawings made with the Hecto pencils and carbons. You can add other colors later with regular crayon pencils. As noted, lettering doesn't have to be reversed when preparing the original. Furthermore, you need not use only the master sheet provided specifically for the Hectograph; just about any strong sheet of paper may be used for the master.

Since you can get several colors at one printing, experiment with Hectograph copies of drawings of flowers, printing the purple, red, or blue blossoms at the same time you print the green leaves. You can add sparkle to a design with a sock of ink from a linoleum cut. Or print on parchment, add a ribbon and seal, and mount on copper foil.

When you have finished using the Hectograph, remove the image with a sponge and hot water, and store it in a cool place until you want it again.

A hectograph print in four colors (all printed at once) mounted on Color-Aid paper as a birthday greeting. By John Carlis.

A hectograph unicorn print in three colors. Edges torn and sent as a party invitation. By John Carlis.

14

Tempera Batik

Batik is a process of printing colors on cloth. Wax, applied to the cloth, acts as a mask, blocking *out* the colors into which the cloth is dipped. Areas where the wax is not applied will *receive* color. *Tempera batik* is a graphic arts method based on the same principle. You cover certain portions of the paper with a water soluble tempera color which acts as a mask in the same way the wax masks out the color. Then the whole page is covered with black waterproof ink; it is allowed to dry. Then you put the page under a faucet, so that the water soluble poster or tempera color will wash off. The tinted or dyed areas that remain will contrast pleasantly with the waterproof black portions of the page which have not received any poster color. This forms a charming color scheme of black and bright colors, rather like that of stained glass, in which a black line supports and surrounds islands of color.

Materials for Tempera Batik

Sheets of irregular, rough surface, student watercolor paper (20″ x 26″, no. 192A A.B. 10¢)
Strathmore charcoal paper in white and colors, (19″ x 25″, no. 261 A.B., 10½¢)
Tracing paper
Soft lead pencils
Jar of white poster paint
Dr. Ph. Martin's Radiant Concentrated Watercolors (lemon and daffodil yellow; turquoise and true blue; crimson and cyclamen; grass green and violet), available at art suppliers in ½ oz. bottles
Muffin tin or a few saucers
Watercolor brushes
Black waterproof ink
Drawing board or piece of plywood or Masonite (about 15″ x 20″)
Roll of gummed tape, 2″ wide
Small sponge
Ruler
Eraser
X-Acto knife

Stretching the Paper

Wet a sheet of 11″ x 14″ watercolor or charcoal paper in a basin of water or under a faucet (Figure 252), and place it horizontally on a board measuring about 15″ x 20″ or a little larger (Figure 253). Cut four strips of gummed tape about 2″ longer than the length and width of your paper (that is, two 14″ strips, and two 17″ strips). Wet one strip of gummed tape at a time and fasten each to the board, the tape overlapping the sheet of paper by about ⅜″ (Figure 254). Press any air bubbles out of the tape with your fingers, but don't worry if the paper itself is wrinkled. Set the sheet aside, and when it is dry, the paper will have stretched drum tight.

Preparing the Design

Using your ruler as a guide, draw a pencil line that divides the paper in half horizontally (Figure 255). Then, measuring the paper inside the tape, draw four vertical lines equidistant from one another. This will give you eight units of about 3¼″ x 5″ each (Figure 256). Now prepare a design this size. Remember to design your card as if it were stained glass, with a black line separating each color. Make a tracing and rub it down eight times on the stretched paper (Figure 257). If you want to make eight different sketches, of course, you may.

Painting the Design

Put some white poster color in each of the cups of a muffin tin or in several saucers. Add a few drops of the brilliant Dr. Martin's Concentrated Watercolors to each cup — providing you with a range of colors — and mix with a watercolor brush. Paint in the designs with the poster colors, keeping the paint thick, and being careful to leave a space between each color (Figure 258).

252. *Wet a sheet of 11"×14" watercolor or charcoal paper in a basin of water or under a faucet.*

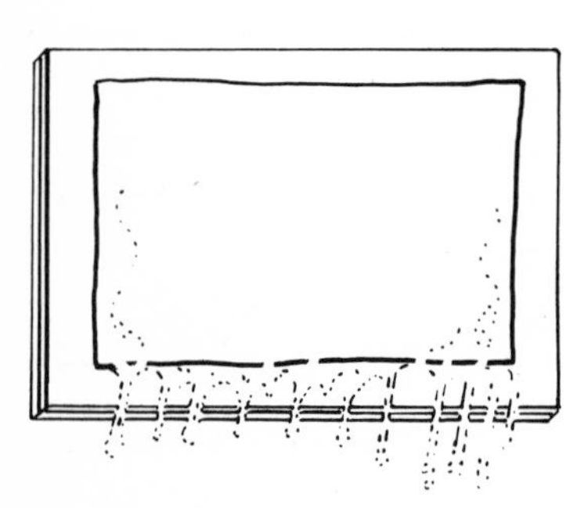

253. *Place the wet sheet on a board measuring about 15"×20".*

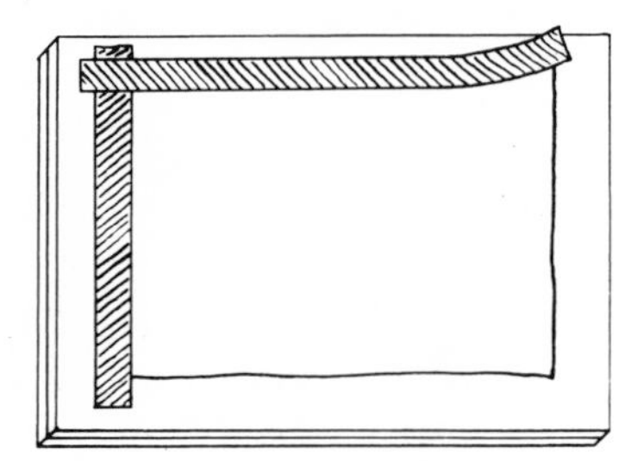

254. *Paste down strips of gummed tape along each edge of the paper, overlapping the sheet by about ⅜".*

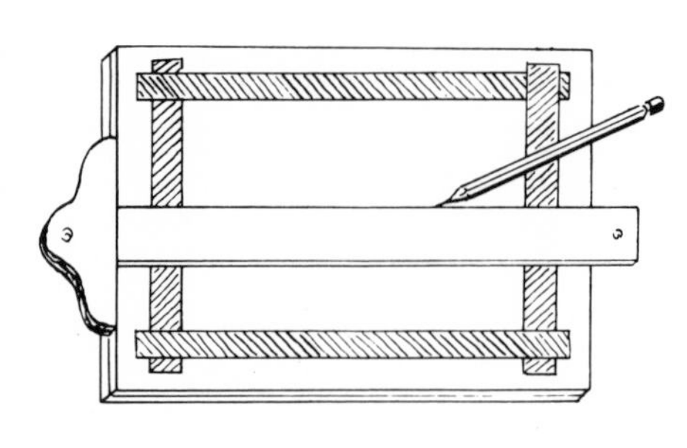

255. *Using the ruler as a guide, divide the paper in half horizontally.*

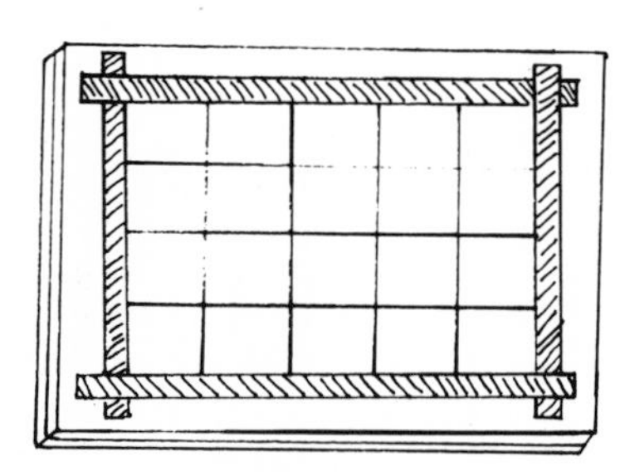

256. *Draw four vertical lines equidistant from one another, giving you eight units, about 3½"×5" each.*

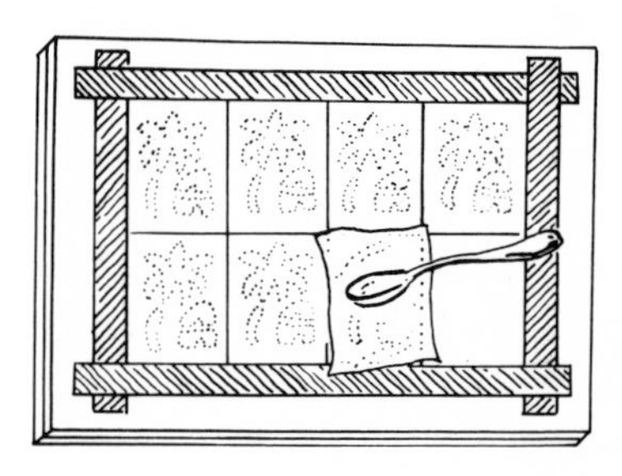

257. *Make a design to fit the 3½"×5" units. Make a tracing and rub it down eight times on the stretched paper.*

258. *Paint in the designs with poster colors. Leave a space between each color in the design.*

Inking and Washing

When your painting is quite dry, pour some black waterproof ink into a saucer. Then, with your biggest water-color brush, flood the entire surface of the painted sheet with the black India ink (Figure 260). Let the ink dry. Take the board to a sink and place it under a faucet, washing off all the poster color (Figure 261). You can nudge off stubborn bits of poster paint with the sponge. The black lines surrounding the tinted color areas should make the card look like stained glass.

259. *Pour some black waterproof ink into a saucer.*

260. *Flood the entire surface of the painted sheet with the India ink.*

261. *After the ink has dried, place the board under a faucet, washing off all the poster color.*

Mounting the Card

Remove the sheet from the board. Cut apart the eight units. They can each be mounted inside the cut-out window mat of a French fold, or tipped onto a slightly larger piece of gold or silver paper before mounting on a larger fold, or onto a box fold of colored paper (Figures 262-264).

262. *Slip the tempera batik under a window mat.*

263. *Or you can tip the tempera batik onto a slightly larger piece of gold or silver paper which you will mount to a larger fold of colored paper.*

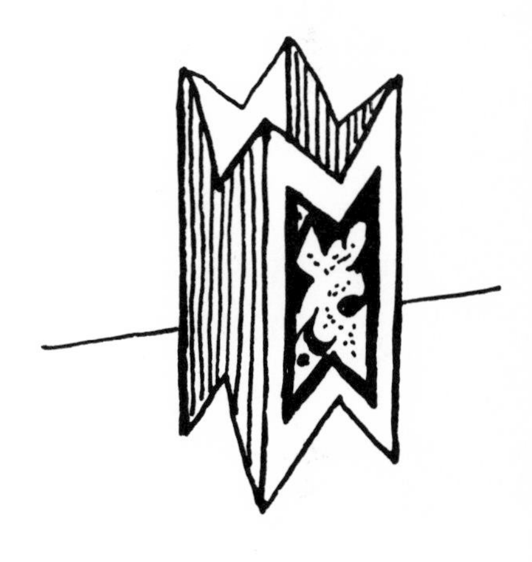

264. *Or you can tip on the tempera batik to a box fold of colored paper.*

Variations

Standard sizes for drawing boards are: 12″ x 17″, 16″ x 21″, 18″ x 24″, and 20″ x 26″. And there are still larger sizes for drafting. The design you make may necessitate dividing your paper into more or fewer units of different dimensions than those I have suggested here.

Notice Figure 265. You can combine potato printing with this method. A stretched sheet of paper is divided into twenty units. Potato halves which have been cut for stamp printing three colors with thick paint are alongside the paper. When the poster paint is dry, the sheet is covered with black waterproof ink, and when the ink is dry, the whole board is washed under a faucet. (Mark the dividing lines with poster color so you will know where to cut apart the finished batiks.)

In subtle yellows and pinks, this tempera batik is an interesting Bon Voyage *card. By John Carlis.*

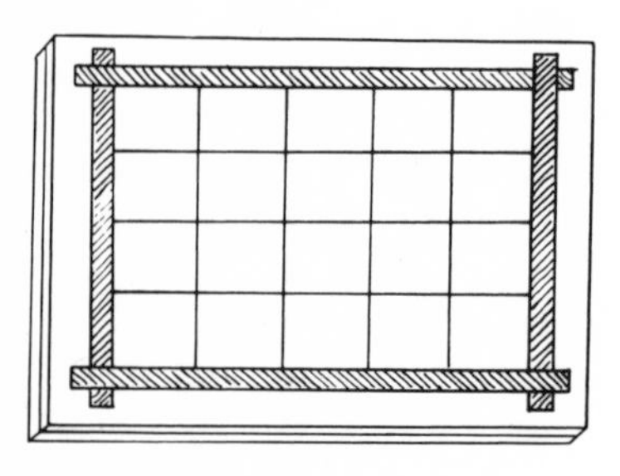

265. *You can combine tempera batiks with other graphic methods; with potato prints, for example.*

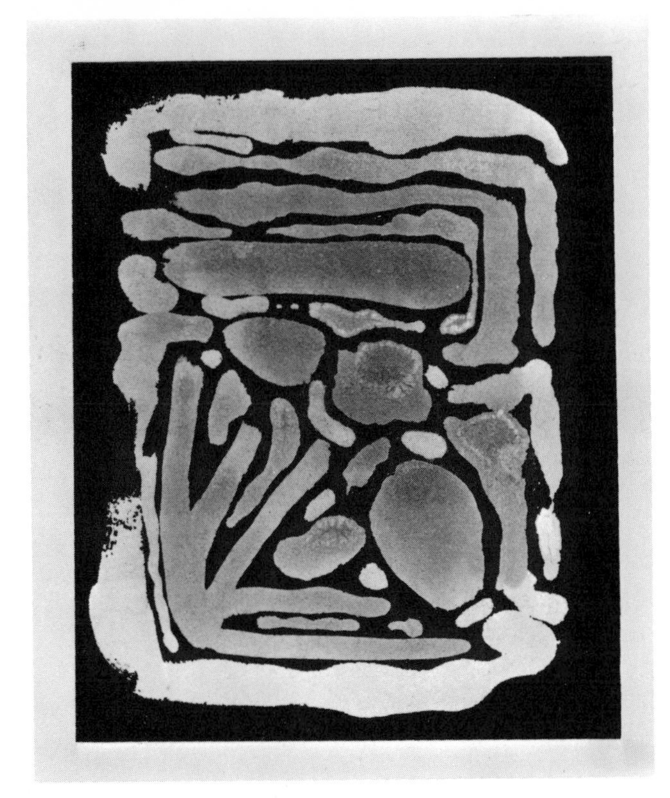

This tempera batik — an accordion fold — gives the impression of having been printed on a black card stock. By John Carlis.

This abstract tempera batik Thank You card takes full advantage of the merits of the process. By John Carlis.

This Thank You card is a tempera batik printed in a fine line from an Indian fabric printing block. By John Carlis.

An Indian fabric printing block was used for this Congratulations card printed in the tempera batik method. By John Carlis.

This tempera batik was painted with poster white on pink paper. An advertisement for a garden restaurant by John Carlis.

15

Collage and 3-D Cards

Twentieth century painters sometimes paste together seemingly unrelated bits of printed matter — newspaper clippings, coupons and tickets, bits of ribbon, pressed flowers — to make a coherent design. This method is called *collage*. Here you mix the real and the fanciful, the old with the new, the trite with the precious. Brandon Memorabilia (see shopping guide) can supply you with all the Victorian scraps you need for $2.00 or $3.00— genuine nineteenth century advertising cards, old gilt paper ornaments, jointed paper dolls, etc. You can also do a bit of rummaging yourself through old newspapers and magazines for interesting bits of copy and art. Combine these with your own stamped prints, blots or rubbings, with monotypes, etchings, or silk screen prints, to make greeting cards that will have a very modern look, regardless of the age of the individual components.

Materials for Collage

Sharp pair of scissors
Lighter fluid or benzine
Elmer's Glue All or any white latex glue
Rubber cement and thinner
thinner
Any kind of scraps for making collages; for example: prints, old and new; old magazines; blueprints; Xerox copies of line illustrations; Victorian scraps; papers of various weights, colors, and textures—foil, suedes, etc.; department store shopping bags; gift wrapping and wallpaper scraps; Goldmark transfer paper; sequins and paper lace; pressed flowers and grasses.

A Word about Rubber Cement

Although rubber cement can't be recommended as a long term adhesive, it has distinct advantages: items pasted down with rubber cement can be easily removed and put down again. To remove an item which has been pasted with rubber cement, simply wash down the entire surface with rubber cement thinner. The dried cement can be rubbed off with your finger or with a "pick-up" (a commercially-made slab of dried rubber cement which will pick up any pieces of the adhesive). For the strongest bond, put one throughly dry surface of cement against another. However, even this will lift apart in several years; rubber cement was developed for advertising agency use and clean, rush work, not for permanence.

Multi-Printed Sheet

Find a printed sheet with designs in repeat (gift wrapping, wallpaper, or a shopping bag). Take a unit like the Macy's shopping bag shown in Figure 267, which has 24 units with each unit shown about four times on each bag. I cut out all the trumpets and recorders. (Or you can cut out wreaths, sleighs, or engines, or whatever design is repeated). Paste these onto a slightly larger piece of gold paper, and then onto a fold of colored paper. (See Figure 268.)

As a message inside, write something appropriate to the design. Here, for example, I wrote: *Big Blast at Our House! Saturday Night, December 15, 9:00.* (See Figure 269.) Other units may be appropriate for other messages: here the little train and the sleigh can be used for *bon voyage* which you can send to your friends lucky enough to be taking a winter holiday. From two or three shopping bags or sheets of decorative paper, you can cut out other units for seasonal children's parties, for anniversary cards, birthday or commencement cards. Depending on how you mount them, these cards can look very expensive and you can be pretty certain no one will receive a card like them.

braid

cut-outs

sequins

ribbons

leaves

266. *Just about any kind of odds and ends are suitable for collage cards.*

267. *A Macy's shopping bag was good material for a collage greeting card.*

268. *Individual items — appropriate to the card — were cut out of the shopping bag and pasted onto slightly larger pieces of gold paper, then pasted again onto a simple fold card.*

BIG BLAST
AT OUR HOUSE
SATURDAY NIGHT
DEC. 15th 9:00 P.M.

269. *An appropriate message was written inside.*

Transfer and Eraser Prints

Think of an idea for a card. Then browse through a newspaper to find one or more illustrations of the idea. Wash lighter fluid or benzene over the newsprint. While the fluid is still wet on the newspaper, take a sheet of white or tinted paper and rub down the design, pressing the sheet against the newspaper with the back of a spoon (Figures 270-272). Arrange these designs in a pattern and paste them down. To augment the illustration, you might cut a gum eraser in a design appropriate to the newsprint, so you can add stamp prints in colored inks from your cut eraser. Add further touches of color with Magic Markers, and write captions in balloons with felt tipped pens. Mount the picture on a fold of colored paper — perhaps a cut-out piece of wallpaper — and add the greeting inside.

270. *Cut out an illustration from the newspaper which expresses your idea.*

271. *Wash lighter fluid over the newspaper clipping.*

272. *Rub down the illustration on your card — while the fluid is still wet.*

273. *To augment the illustration, you might add an eraser print.*

274. *Add further touches of color with Magic Markers and mount the illustration on a fold of colored paper, perhaps cut from a sheet of wallpaper.*

Making a Look-Through Box Fold Card

First choose your envelope. Then lay out a rectangle which measures about ¼″ smaller all around than the face of the envelope (Figure 275). Allow an inch or 1¼″ for an end. Take a sheet of stiff paper or paper board which is either plain or one you have decoratively printed. Lay out a front and back of the same dimension, and two ends of equal dimensions, plus another end that folds over and pastes down (Figure 276).

Make sure you fold with the grain of the paper (see page 23). Experiment with a small piece; if the fold is made easily and cleanly, you've folded it with the grain. If it's *necessary* to fold against the grain, score the line lightly with a blade or sharp point before folding.

Now paste the end of your box fold so that it will stand up (Figure 277). Cut a hole in the face—make the hole square or make the hole decorative in contour if you like—so that you will be able to look through to the inside back of the box fold. On the back "wall," paste a rose, hibiscus, or a bunch of lilacs (which you can cut from a nursery catalog, from wallpaper, or from gift wrapping scraps). Perhaps you've run across a series of prints of antique cars you'd like to use—or a snapshot, a lettered greeting, a feather, tinsel, a stamp or seal (see Figures 276-282).

Now comes the assembly line fun. On the face of each box, paste a print of a column, a tree, or a chimney. If your design calls for an eye or an asterisk, an exclamation point or a finial, try pasting on a colored sequin. You can use a hand colored transfer

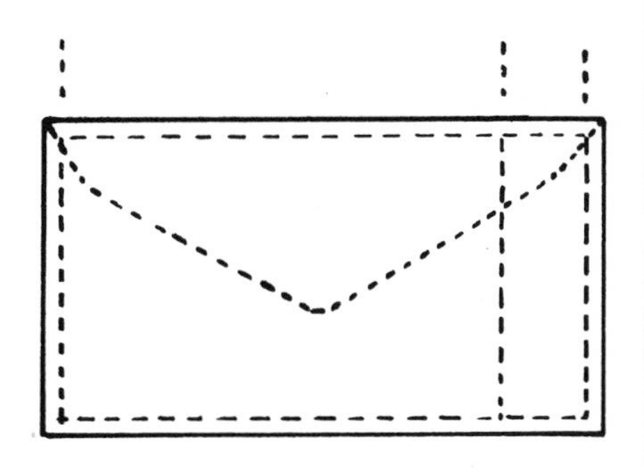

275. *Lay out a rectangle of paper as a face and an end which is about ¼″ smaller all around than the face of the envelope.*

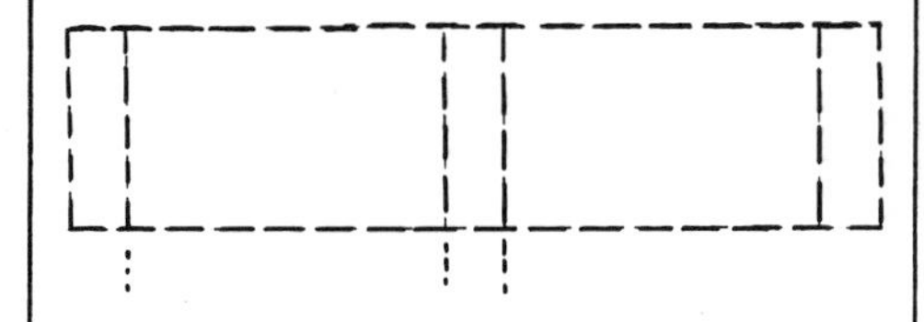

276. *Now cut a strip of paper board, showing a front and back and two ends—plus an extra end to fold over and paste down.*

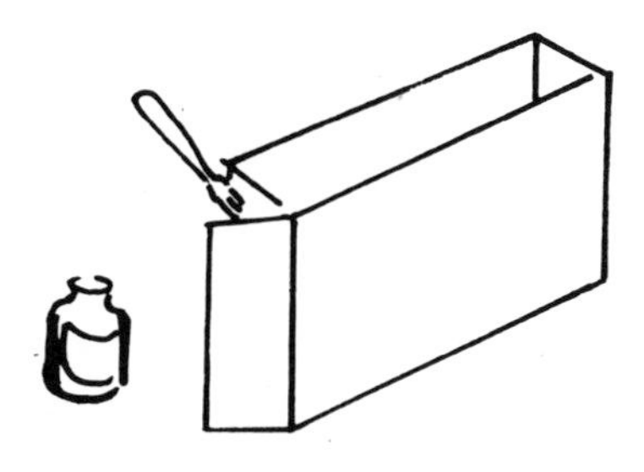

277. *Paste the end of the box fold so that it will stand up.*

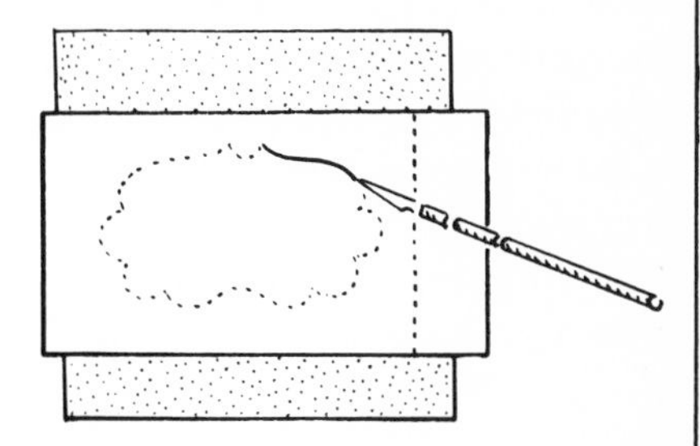

278. *Slip a piece of scrap paper board inside the fold and cut a hole in the face of the box fold. The opening can be square or decorative as shown here.*

279. *On the back wall, paste some item of decorative interest.*

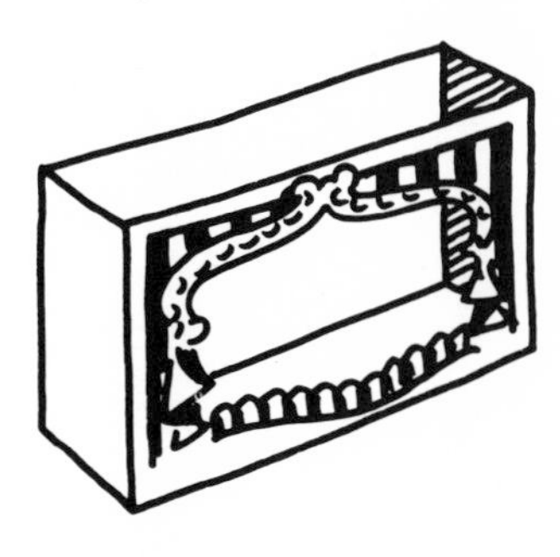

280. *On the face of the box, paste decorative prints.*

print or a tempera batik. Add a miniature flag or a bit of silk braid. Stand back and admire the sparkle. Fold and insert the card in the envelope, imagining the pleasure you will give the receivers when they stand up your card on the mantlepiece!

281. *Here's a variation of the same idea.*

282. *From magazines you can cut out the casement window, the plant, and the bay scene and make this stage set.*

Variations

There are many things you can use in collage and 3-D cards: doll patterns, gala boats and paper hats, sun burst cut-outs, and pop-out greetings. An accordion fold house can be developed in a great many ways for different occasions. You can also cut out the shapes of prints you've made on heavy paper, punch the card, and run a cord through the hole, to make a hanging ornament (Figure 283). These ideas needn't be limited to Christmas. Paper toys as hanging ornaments can be sent to children throughout the year; psychedelic and astrological signs sent as hanging greeting cards are also amusing. A cut-out and punched get well card can be hung from a light cord or from a bed post.

The important thing is to get into the habit of having on hand the materials you feel most at home with and to produce batches of cards regularly. The telephone and television may have replaced the letter, but nothing in this computerized age can replace the memorabilia we've produced with our own hands. Furthermore — as I've tried to point out — your greeting cards need not be highly finished works of art. *Hope Your Christmas is a Knock-Out* in big, bold letters — showing boxers in the ring — was made by a youngster from a very crude linocut. This terracotta sporting print on rough paper had more dash than any other card I received that year. "Hearts hang on the little pegs of our imperfections," and the unsophisticated greeting can be every bit as inspired as the virtuoso performance. What matters is the postman delivering a print or a sketch — sporting or religious, funny or romantic — that reminds us we've been remembered. So keep your glue pot handy, your pencils and scissors sharp. And have fun!

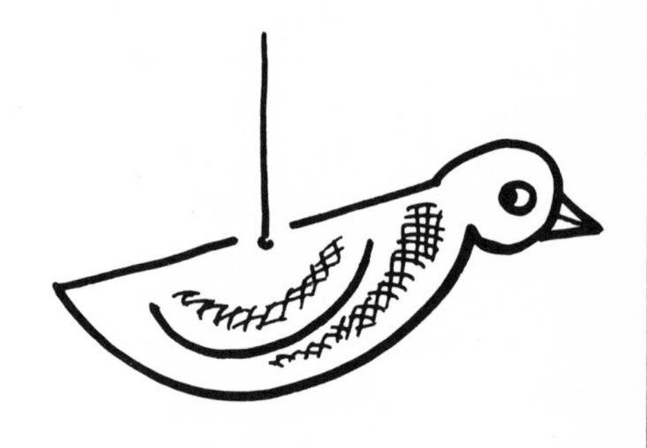

283. *Cut-outs can make excellent hanging ornaments.*

284. *Here's a tree, easily assembled, that makes an imaginative card.*

The design was drawn over an offset tracing and the tree assembled by attaching it to a simple box fold as described in Chapter 15. By John Carlis.

This artist cut out a color reproduction of a painting by Vermeer, added a bold border and an appropriate message — with a felt heart to suggest Valentine's Day. Mounted on white card stock. By Marcia Zanphir.

Onto a sheet of colored paper, the artist adhered dried pressed flowers, weeds, and feathers, then covered the pieces with a clear contact paper (no glue is needed). Mounted in this way, the foliage appears to be painted. By Mrs. Herbert Bauer.

A simple linocut made by a child, mounted onto card stock, can be as imaginative a card as any you'd hope to receive. By Steve Boduarchuk.

Made out of a page of the Sunday paper, this New Year's card suggests all the spirit of the holiday. Betty and Cal Anderson.

Twenty-eight pieces of paper were glued onto a sheet of construction paper to give the effect of a third dimension. By Catalda.

To create this border "doorway," the artist colored a photostat. Through the doors, he placed an offset tracing of a crib: an ideal birth announcement. By John Carlis.

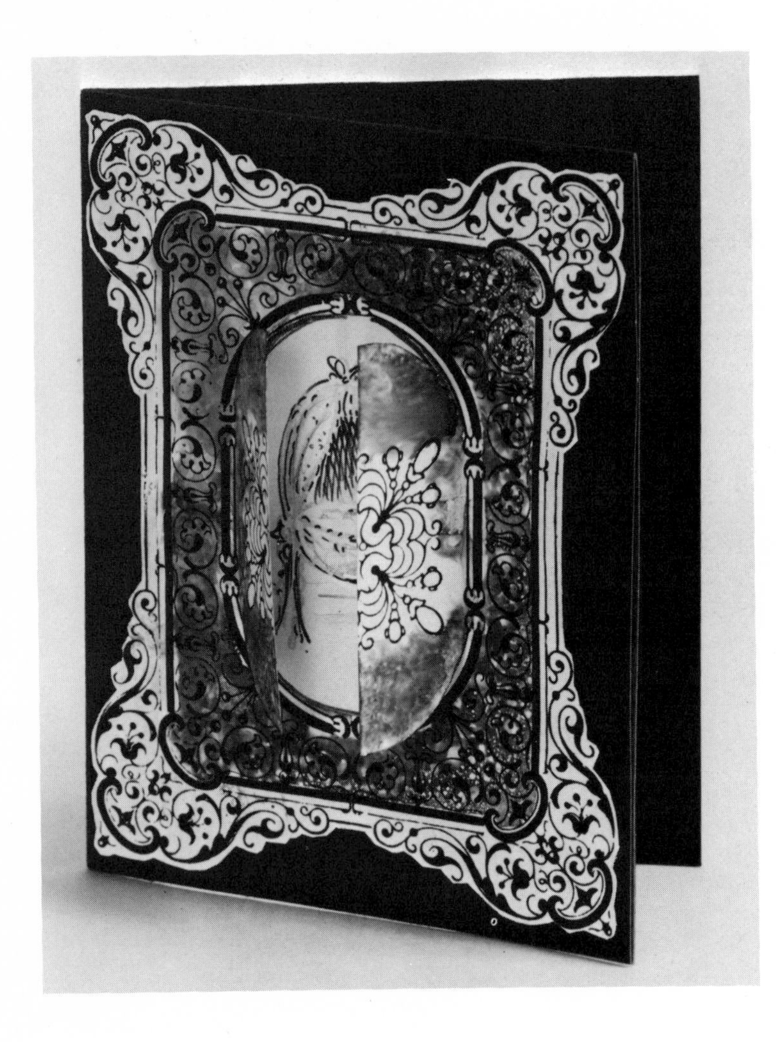

Cancelled postage stamps were cut and applied to a card stock with Duco Cement. Water color details were added later. By Mabel M. Linkous.

Using household glue, the artist applied natural ferns and leaves to a sheet of rice paper and added watercolor details. By Celia Hamilton.

In this card, a simple line drawing was pasted onto a sheet of green paper. Gold tips were added to suggest the rooftops and doorways. By John Carlis.

A Victorian cupid pasted onto a paper doily adds a dainty touch to Valentine's Day. By Marcia Zanphir

Combining Victorian scraps with a rubbing (the border around the cat) and gift wrapping paper, produces an imaginative birthday greeting. By John Carlis.

Paper of different colors was used to create a pictorial element here. The motif is ideal for a child's birthday card. By Marcia Zanphir.

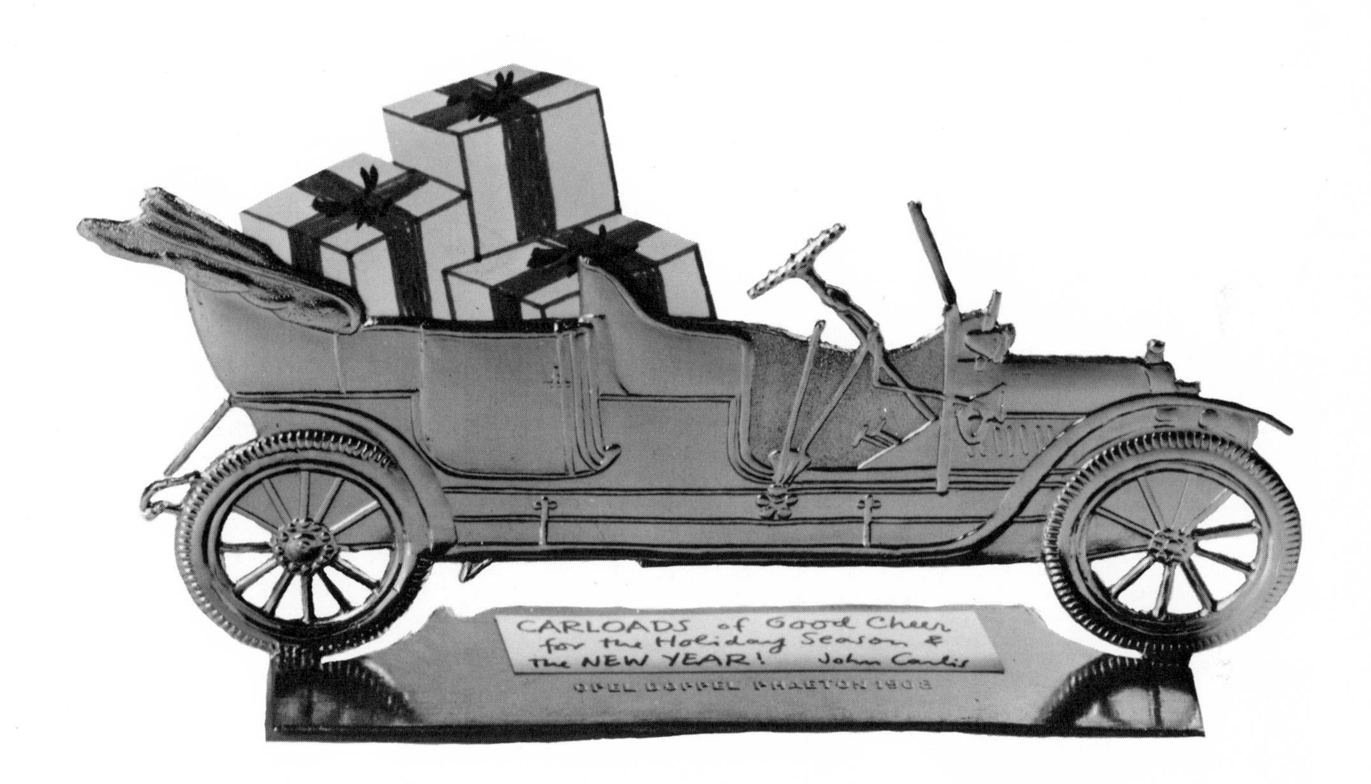

What started out to be an advertisement for an automobile, was converted into a handsome three dimensional card: "Carloads of Good Cheer for the Holiday Season." By John Carlis.

Shopping Guide

Virtually all the materials mentioned in this book may be obtained from the art suppliers listed in classified telephone directories across the United States and Canada. A complete catalog, published by one of America's largest art supply distributors — Arthur Brown and Bro., Inc. — includes photographic and silk screen supplies and is available to those who visit or write to Arthur Brown and Bro., Inc., 2 West 46 Street, New York, New York 10036.

Specialty Papers

Andrews, Nelson, Whitehead, Boise
7 Laight Street
New York, New York

Wallpaper

Sears Roebuck & Co.
(branches all over the U.S.A.)
Montgomery Ward
(branches all over the U.S.A.)

Victorian Scraps

Brandon Memorabilia
13 East 53 Street
New York, New York 10022

Harrower House of Découpage
River Road
Upper Black Eddy
Bucks County, Pennsylvania

Plastics

Industrial Plastics Supply Co.
342 Canal Street
New York, New York

Plastic Snowflakes

Allied Display Materials
241 West 23 Street
New York, New York

Duplicators

Mimeo Manufacturing Co., Inc.
401 Broadway
New York, New York

Goldsmith's
77 Nassau Street
New York, New York 10038

Copymate machines at any major department or stationery store

Beads, Sequins, Jewels, Plastic Novelties

Sol Kahaner and Bro.
55 West 38 Street
New York, New York 10018

Max Millinery Center
13 West 38 Street
New York, New York 10018

Dennison Manufacturing Company
370 Lexington Avenue
New York, New York 10017

Consult your classified directory for millinery suppliers

Index

Edited by Susan E. Meyer
Designed by James Craig
Composed in ten point Palatino by Noera-Rayns Studio Inc.
Printed and Bound by The Haddon Craftsmen, Inc.